CHINA

FOREIGN LANGUAGES PRESS

General Supervisor: **Zhou Mingwei**

Chief Editors: **Zhou Mingwei, Guo Changjian, Huang Youyi**

Deputy Chief Editors: **Li Zhenguo, Hu Kaimin**

Executive Chief Editor: **Xu Mingqiang**

English Editors: **Paul White, Han Qingyue**

English Translators: **Wang Qin, Jiang Xiaoning, Wang Wei, Liu Kuijuan,**

Yan Jing, Qu Lei, Feng Xin

First Edition 2011

ISBN 978-7-119-07180-0

© Foreign Languages Press Co. Ltd, Beijing, China, 2011

Published by
Foreign Languages Press Co. Ltd
24 Baiwanzhuang Road, Beijing 100037, China
http://www.flp.com.cn
E-mail: flp@cipg.org.cn

Distributed by
China International Book Trading Corporation
35 Chegongzhuang Xilu, Beijing 100044, China
P.O. Box 399, Beijing, China

Printed in the People's Republic of China

Foreword

China is an ancient country possessing many world-class heritage sites such as the Great Wall, the Terracotta Warriors and Horses of Qin Shi Huang, the Palace Museum and the Suzhou gardens, as well as world-famous ancient luminaries including the great educator Confucius and the author of *Art of War*, Sun Wu, among many others.

Sixty-two years have passed since the founding ceremony of the People's Republic of China on the Tiananmen Square in 1949. The People's Republic has shown its resolute vitality to the whole world. In particular, bold endeavors through over 30 years of reform and opening up have helped China's economy realize steady and rapid growth. China has achieved a total transformation from silent isolation to a remarkable rise which has attracted the world's attention, focusing not only on China's ancient culture, but also toward its present and future.

China is a primer to help international readers acquire a better understanding of China. While maintaining certain basic historical facts and general information, it offers the latest facts and figures on every facet of China, including its international contacts, cultural exchanges, economic growth, environmental protection, developments in science and technology, social progress, and improvements of people's livelihood, with the aim of assisting readers toward a wider and deeper knowledge of China.

We hope you will find this book useful.

Contents

46
Administrative Divisions and Cities

China is divided into 23 provinces, five autonomous regions, four municipalities directly under the Central Government and two special administrative regions.

66
Population and Ethnicity

China has the world's largest population, with 56 ethnic groups enjoying harmonious coexistence. They live together over vast areas, with some living in compact communities in small areas. *Hanyu* (Chinese language) is the most commonly used language in China, while most of the 55 minority peoples have their own languages.

82
Political System and State Structure

China's political system basically consists of, under the unified leadership of the CPC, the people's congress system, the multiparty cooperation and political consultation system, and the regional ethnic autonomy system.

98
Foreign Relations

Foreign Policy / Friendship with Neighboring Countries /
Cooperation with Developing Countries /
Cooperation with Major Countries /
Actively Participating in Multilateral Affairs

Since 1949, the People's Republic of China has unswervingly pursued an independent foreign policy of peace. It is committed to developing friendship and cooperation with neighboring countries, developing countries and the major powers on the basis of the Five Principles of Peaceful Coexistence.

114
Economy

Economic Development / Economic System /
Economic Structure / From Opening Up Coastal Areas to
All-around Opening Up / Coordinated Development
of All Regions and Comprehensive Reform / Agriculture /
Industry / Service Industries

After more than 30 years of reform and opening up, a socialist market economy has been basically established in China, and an omni-directional pattern of opening up which is wide-ranging, multi-level with priorities has taken shape.

156
Environmental Protection

Laws and Systems for Environmental Protection /
New Changes in Environmental Protection /
Addressing Climate Change / Air Pollution Control /
Water Pollution Control / Protection of Forest Resources /
Nature Reserves / Protecting Endangered Animals and Plants /
ENGOs / International Cooperation

Many places in China were densely wooded and had beautiful landscapes in the past, but due to such factors as large population and a backward economy, those places have seen vegetation deterioration, soil erosion and even desertification.

Location of the People's Republic of China

North America

South America

A bird's-eye-view of the Qinghai-Tibet Plateau

Land and Resources

Seen from above, the Chinese continent is shaped like four broad steps descending from the Qinghai-Tibet Plateau over 4,000 m above sea level on average in the west to the continental shelf zone less than 200 m deep in the east. The land area of China almost equals that of the whole of Europe. But the landform differs greatly from one place to another, as do resources.

Land Area

Located in the eastern part of the Asian continent, on the western shore of the Pacific, the People's Republic of China has a land area of 9.6 million sq km, and is the third largest country in the world, next only to Russia and Canada. From north to south, the territory of China stretches from the center of the Heilong River north of the town of Mohe to the Zengmu Reef at the southernmost tip of the Nansha Islands, a length of 5,500 km. From east to west, the country extends from the confluence of the Heilong and Wusuli rivers to the Pamir Mountains, spanning 5,200 km.

With land boundaries totaling about 22,800 km, China is bordered by the Democratic People's Republic of Korea (DPRK) to the east; Mongolia to the north; Russia to the northeast; Kazakhstan, Kyrgyzstan and Tajikistan to the northwest; Afghanistan, Pakistan, India, Nepal and Bhutan to the west and southwest; and Myanmar, Laos and Vietnam to the south. Across the seas to the east and southeast are the Republic of Korea (ROK), Japan, the Philippines, Brunei, Malaysia and Indonesia.

China's mainland coastline measures approximately 18,000 km, with a flat topography and many excellent harbors, most of which are ice-free all year round. The Chinese mainland is flanked to the east and south by the Bohai, Yellow, East China and South China seas, with a total maritime area of about 4.7 million sq km. The Bohai Sea is China's continental sea, while the Yellow, East China and South China seas are marginal seas of the Pacific.

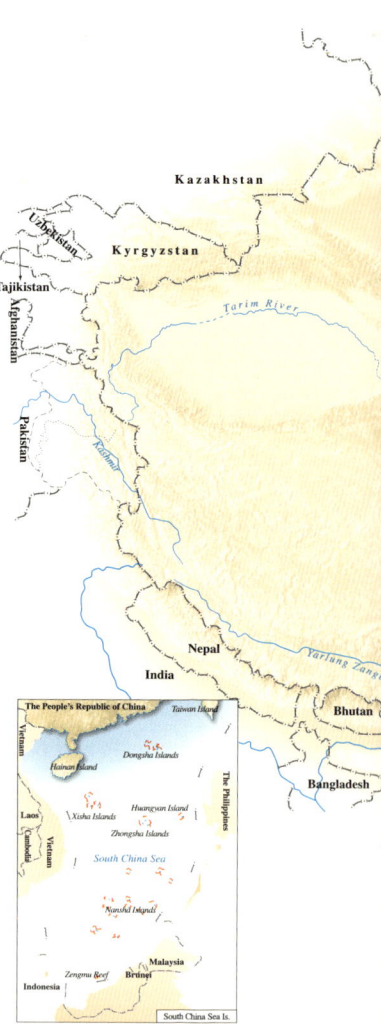

Russia

Mongolia

Heilong River

Xingkai Lake

Beijing

The People's Republic of China

Bohai Sea

D.P.R. Korea

R.O. Korea

Yellow River

Yellow River

Yellow Sea

Japan

Yangtze River

Yangtze River

East China Sea

Chiwei Island

Diaoyu Island

Lancang River

Myanmar

Pearl River

Penghu Islands

Taiwan Island

Taiwan Straits

Vietnam

Dongsha Islands

Laos

Thailand

Hainan Island

South China Sea

The Philippines

Thailand

A total of 7,600 islands and islets dot China's territorial waters. The largest of these, with an area of about 36,000 sq km, is Taiwan, followed by Hainan with an area of 34,000 sq km. The Diaoyu and Chiwei islands, located to the northeast of Taiwan Island, are China's easternmost islands. The many islands, islets, reefs and shoals in the South China Sea, known collectively as the South China Sea Islands, are China's southernmost island group. They are called Dongsha, Xisha, Zhongsha or Nansha Islands, according to their geographical locations.

Mountain Ranges

China has nine mountain ranges with an average elevation of 6,000 m and above, and over 20 ranges with an average elevation of 4,000 m and above. The Himalayas, the highest mountain range, extending over the border of China with India, Nepal and other countries, contains over 30 peaks of 7,300 m or higher and 11 peaks of 8,000 m or higher in elevation. Soaring 8,844.43 m above sea level is Mount Qomolangma, the world's highest peak and the main peak of the Himalayas. The Kunlun mountain range, averaging 5,500 m to 6,000 m in elevation, runs from west to east across the Xinjiang Uyghur and Tibet autonomous regions, and Qinghai and Sichuan provinces. Some 2,500 km

Topography of China

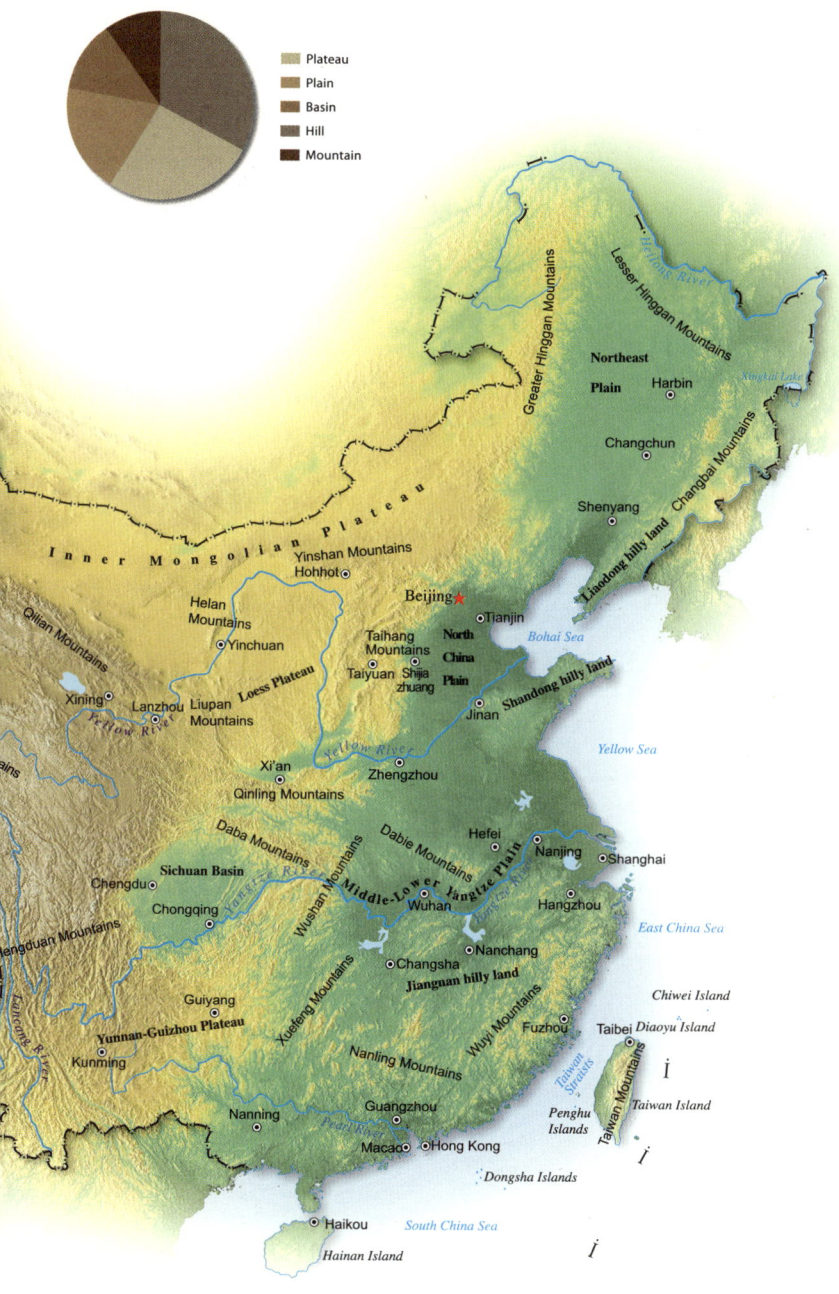

Plateau
Plain
Basin
Hill
Mountain

Heilong River

Lesser Hinggan Mountains

Greater Hinggan Mountains

Northeast Plain

Harbin

Xingkai Lake

Changchun

Changbai Mountains

Shenyang

Inner Mongolian Plateau

Yinshan Mountains

Hohhot

Liaodong hilly land

Qilian Mountains

Helan Mountains

Beijing ★

Tianjin

Bohai Sea

Yinchuan

Taihang Mountains

North China Plain

Xining

Lanzhou

Loess Plateau

Liupan Mountains

Taiyuan

Shijia zhuang

Jinan

Shandong hilly land

Yellow River

Yellow River

Zhengzhou

Yellow Sea

Xi'an

Qinling Mountains

Daba Mountains

Dabie Mountains

Hefei

Nanjing

Shanghai

Chengdu

Sichuan Basin

Wushan Mountains

Middle-Lower Yangtze Plain

Wuhan

Hangzhou

Chongqing

Yangtze River

East China Sea

engduan Mountains

Changsha

Nanchang

Guiyang

Xuefeng Mountains

Jiangnan hilly land

Chiwei Island

Yunnan-Guizhou Plateau

Nanling Mountains

Wuyi Mountains

Fuzhou

Taibei

Diaoyu Island

Kunming

Lancang River

Taiwan Straits

Taiwan Mountains

Nanning

Guangzhou

Pearl River

Penghu Islands

Taiwan Island

Macao

Hong Kong

Dongsha Islands

Haikou

South China Sea

Hainan Island

Sunset over Mount Qomolangma

Mount Tai

long and 200 km to 500 km wide, the Kunlun is the longest range in China. The Thanglha and Qinling mountains are also notable for their height and size. The Thanglha range on the central Qinghai-Tibet Plateau, averaging 6,000 m above sea level, is the source of the Yangtze, China's longest river. The Qinling Mountains, extending west to east from eastern Gansu Province to western Henan Province, with average elevations of 2,000 m to 3,000 m, make up a geographical division line for north and south China's differing cultures and climates.

Plateaus

China has four major plateaus. The Qinghai-Tibet Plateau, consisting of all of Qinghai and Tibet and parts of Gansu, Yunnan and Sichuan, is the world's highest plateau. Averaging 4,000 m above sea level, the Qinghai-Tibet Plateau is considered the "roof of the world." The Inner Mongolian Plateau in the Inner Mongolia Autonomous Region is flanked by grasslands in the east and desert in the west. The Loess Plateau, comprising all or parts of six provinces and autonomous regions, including Shaanxi and Shanxi, is thickly covered with loess and suffers from serious water and soil loss. The Yunnan-Guizhou Plateau, covering eastern Yunnan Province and most of Guizhou Province, has typical karst topography.

Plains

China's three largest plains are the Northeast Plain, of more than 350,000 sq km, the North China Plain, of about 300,000 sq km in central China, and the Middle-Lower Yangtze Plain, of around 200,000 sq km and with a low flat terrain formed by alluvia from the Yangtze River.

Basins

China has four major basins. The Tarim Basin in Xinjiang is the largest and contains China's largest and the world's second largest desert, the Taklimakan Desert. The Junggar Basin is located in the same region. The Qaidam Basin in Qinghai Province is the highest basin in China, while the Sichuan Basin in Sichuan Province is the wettest.

Rivers

China abounds in rivers. More than 1,500 rivers each drain 1,000 sq km or larger areas. As a result, China is rich in waterpower resources, leading the world in hydropower potential, with reserves of 680 million kw. Due to its large population, however, China's per capita volume of water resources is equal to only one quarter of the world's average.

China's rivers can be categorized as belonging to exterior and interior systems. The catchment area of the exterior rivers that empty into the oceans accounts for 64% of the country's total land area. That of the interior rivers that flow into inland lakes or disappear into deserts or salt marshes makes up the other 36%.

The Yangtze, 6,300 km long, is the longest river in China, and the third longest in the world. Passing through high mountains and deep valleys, the upper section of the Yangtze River is abundant in water resources. The Yangtze is a transportation artery linking west and east, its navigation benefiting from excellent natural channels. The Yellow River is the second longest river in China, with a length of 5,464 km. The Yellow River valley is one of the birthplaces of ancient Chinese civilization. The Heilong River is a major river in northeast China, with a total length

The lower reaches of the
Yarlung Zangbo River

Crossing the Yarlung Zangbo River by ropeway

of 4,350 km, of which 3,101 km is in Chinese territory. The Pearl River, 2,214 km long, is a major river in south China. In southern Xinjiang the Tarim River's 2,179 km makes it China's longest interior river.

In addition to rivers bestowed by nature, China has a famous manmade waterway — the Grand Canal, running from Beijing in the north to Zhejiang Province's Hangzhou in the south. Work began on the Grand Canal as early as in the fifth century BC. It links five major rivers: Haihe, Yellow, Huaihe, Yangtze and Qiantang. With a total length of 1,801 km, the Grand Canal is the longest as well as the oldest artificial waterway in the world.

Lakes

China's territory includes numerous lakes. Most of those lakes are found on the Middle-Lower Yangtze Plain and the Qinghai-Tibet Plateau. Freshwater lakes such as Poyang, Dongting, Taihu and Hongze mostly lie in the former area, while in the latter are found saltwater lakes such as Qinghai, Nam Co and Serling Co. Poyang Lake, in northern Jiangxi Province, has an area of 3,583 sq km, making it the largest of its kind. Northeast Qinghai Province's Qinghai Lake, with an area of 4,583 sq km, is the largest saltwater lake in China.

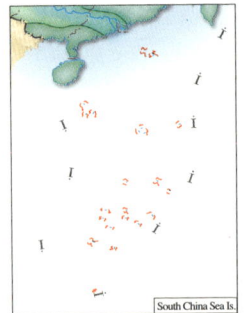

South China Sea Is.

Climate

Most of China lies in the northern temperate zone, characterized by distinctive seasons and a continental monsoon climate, which is well

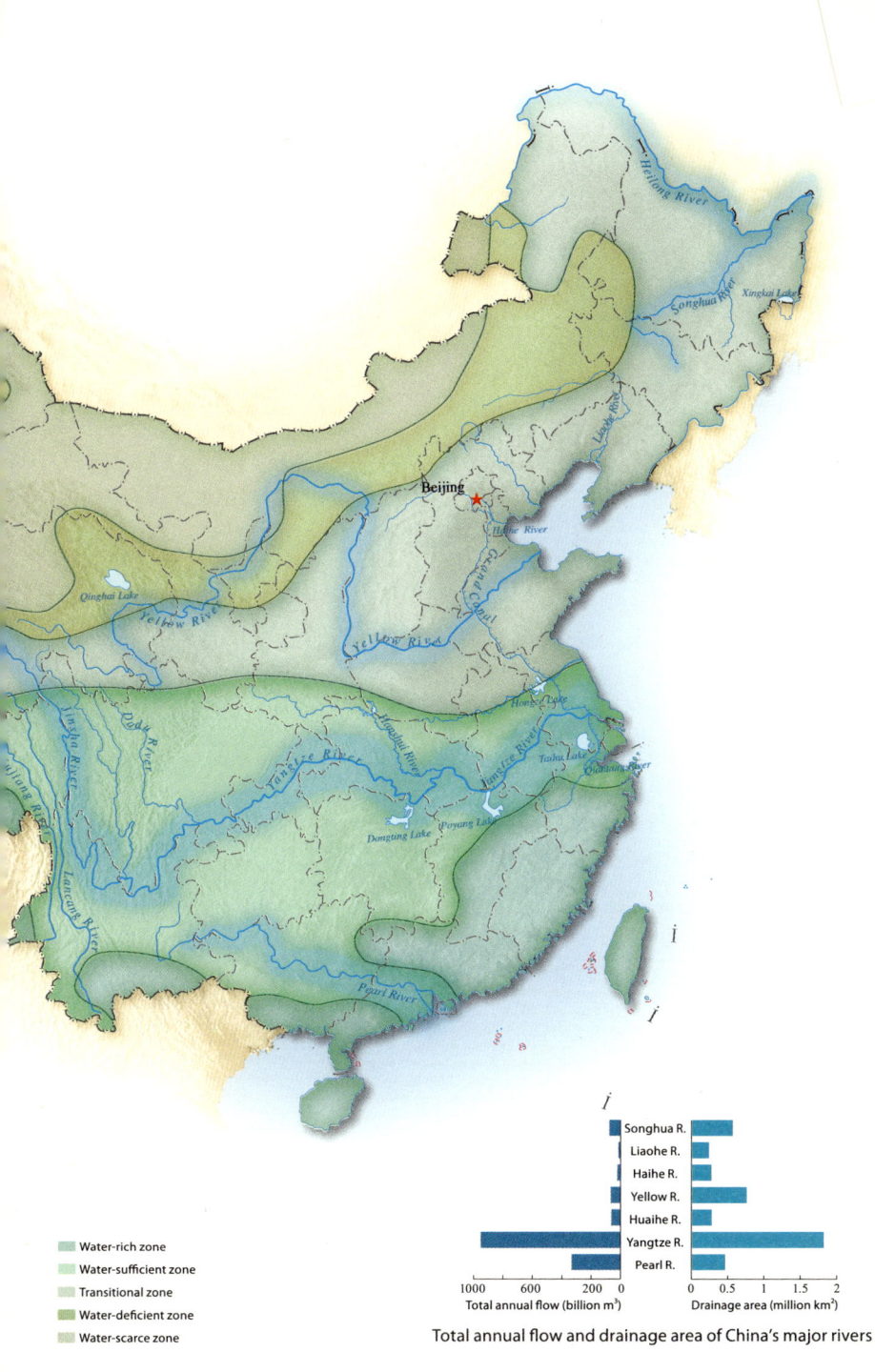

Total annual flow and drainage area of China's major rivers

- Water-rich zone
- Water-sufficient zone
- Transitional zone
- Water-deficient zone
- Water-scarce zone

suited for habitation. From September to April of the following year, the dry and cold winter monsoons blow from Siberia and the Mongolian Plateau, resulting in cold and dry winters, and great differences between the temperatures of north and south China. From April to September, warm and humid summer monsoons blow from the seas in the east and south, resulting in overall high temperatures and abundant rainfall, and little temperature difference between north and south China. In terms of temperature, the country can be sectored from south to north into equatorial, tropical, subtropical, warm-temperate, temperate, and cold-temperate zones. Precipitation gradually declines from the southeast coast to the northwest inlands, with the average annual precipitation varying greatly from place to place. In the southeastern coastal areas, it is over 1,500 mm; while in northwestern areas it drops to below 200 mm.

Sketch Map Showing Rainfall Distribution

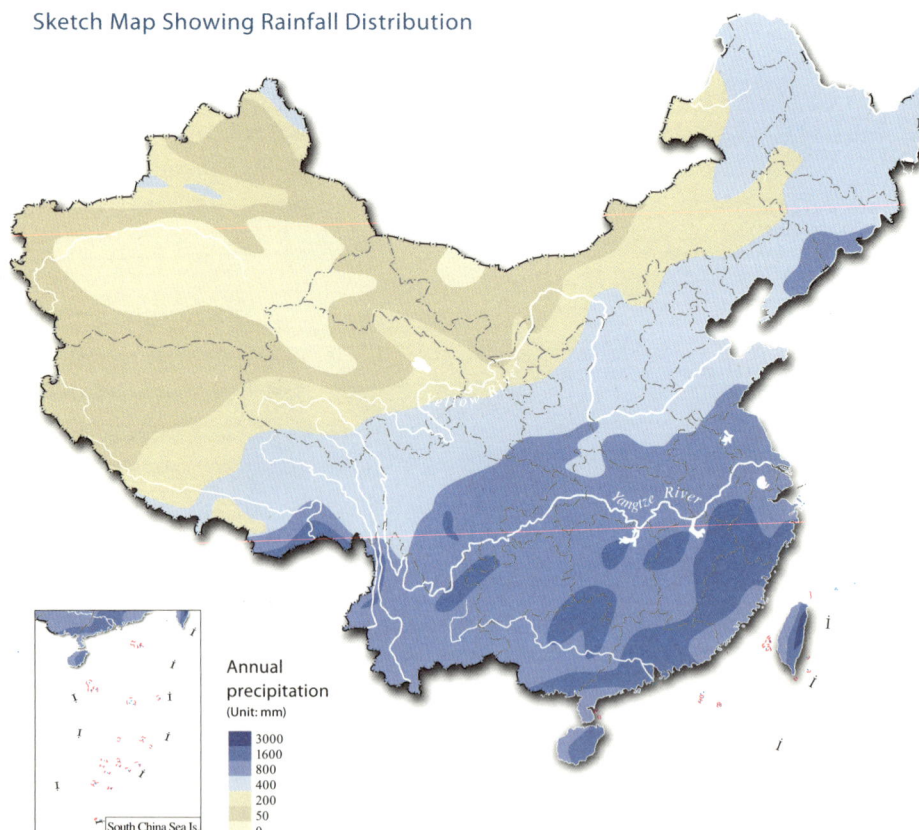

Annual precipitation
(Unit: mm)

3000
1600
800
400
200
50
0

South China Sea Is.

Sketch Map Showing Climate Categories

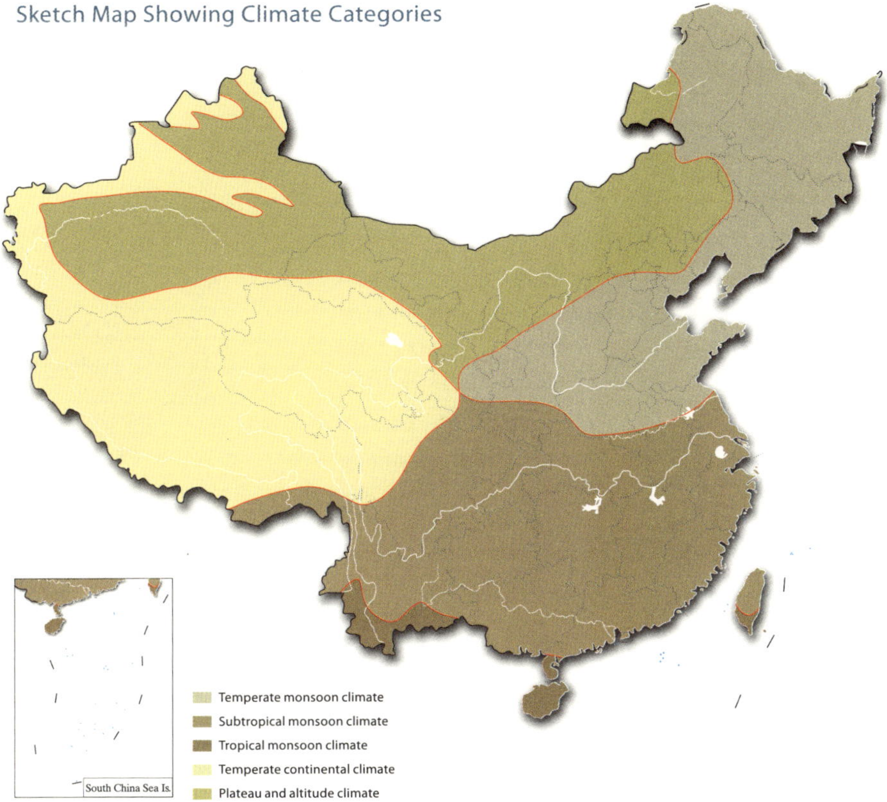

South China Sea Is.

Temperate monsoon climate
Subtropical monsoon climate
Tropical monsoon climate
Temperate continental climate
Plateau and altitude climate

Tropical scenery of Hainan Island

Snow in northeast China

Land

Cultivated land, forests, grasslands, deserts and tidelands are distributed widely across China. Cultivated land is mainly located in east China; grasslands are mainly located in the north and the west; and forests mainly in the remote northeast and southwest. In China today, about 121.72 million ha of land is cultivated; grasslands cover an area of nearly 400 million ha, or 41.7% of China's total land size; and forests cover about 195.45 million ha, with the forest coverage rate at 20.36%. China's cultivated lands, forests and grasslands are among the world's largest in terms of sheer area. But due to China's large population, the per capita areas of cultivated land, forest and grassland are small, especially in the case of cultivated land, which is less than one third of the world's average.

Sketch Map Showing Forest
and Pasture Areas

Northeast China Area

Inner Mongolia and
Great Wall Area

Loess Plateau Area

Area of Yellow
and Huaihe Rivers

Southwest China Area

Area of Middle and
Lower Reaches
of Yangtze River

South China Area

South China Sea Is.

Cultivated Lands

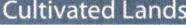

China's cultivated lands are mainly located on the Northeast Plain, the North China Plain, the Middle-Lower Yangtze Plain, the Pearl River Delta, and the Sichuan Basin. The Northeast Plain abounds in wheat, corn, soybean, sorghum, flax and sugar beet. The North China Plain is planted with wheat, corn, millet and cotton. The Middle-Lower Yangtze Plain's low, flat terrain and many lakes and rivers make it particularly suitable for paddy rice and freshwater fish, hence its designation as a "land of fish and rice." This area also produces large quantities of tea and silkworms. The Sichuan Basin in all four seasons is green with crops, including paddy rice, rapeseed and sugarcane, making it known as a "land of plenty." The Pearl River Delta abounds in paddy rice, with two or three harvests a year.

Natural Pasturelands

Grasslands in China stretch several thousand kilometers from the northeast to the southwest, including quite a few centers of animal husbandry. The Inner Mongolia Prairie is China's largest natural pastureland, and home to the famed Sanhe horses, Sanhe cattle and Mongolian sheep. The natural pasturelands north and south of the Tianshan Mountains in Xinjiang are ideal for stockbreeding. World-renowned Ili horses and Xinjiang fine-wool sheep are raised here.

Natural Forests

The Greater Hinggan, Lesser Hinggan and Changbai mountain ranges in the northeast are China's largest natural forest areas. Major tree species found here include conifers and broadleaf trees. Major tree species in the southwest include dragon spruce, fir and Yunnan pine. Often called a "kingdom of plants," Xishuangbanna in the south of Yunnan Province is a rare tropical broadleaf forest area in China, playing host to more than 5,000 plant species.

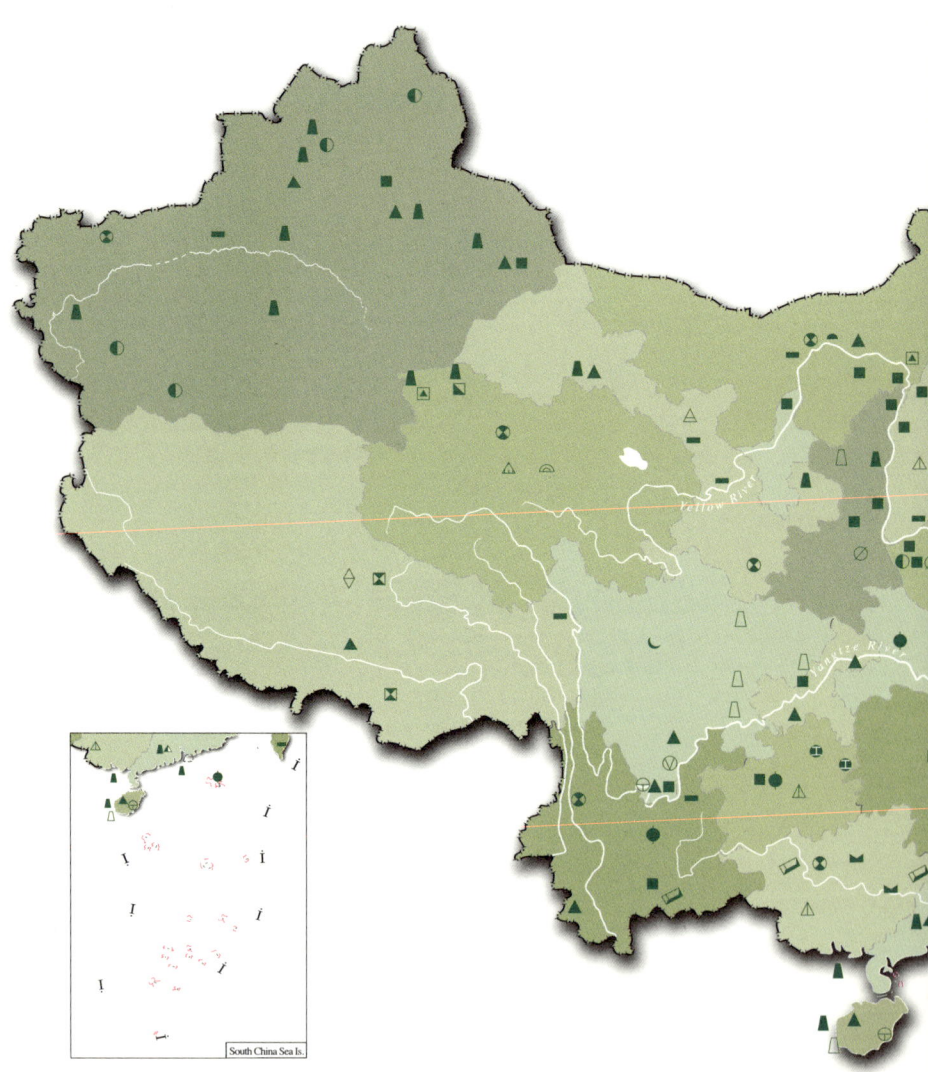

South China Sea Is.

Mineral Resources

China is rich in mineral resources, and all the world's known minerals can be found here. To date, geologists have confirmed reserves of 158 kinds of minerals, putting China third in the world in terms of total reserves. Reserves of major mineral resources, such as coal, iron, copper, aluminum, stibium, molybdenum, manganese, tin, lead, zinc and mercury, are front-ranking in the world. China's basic coal reserves total 326.126 billion tons, mainly distributed in northwest and north China, with Shanxi, Shaanxi, Xinjiang and Inner Mongolia heading the field. China's 22.364 billion tons of basic iron ore reserves are mainly distributed in the northeast, north and southwest. The national reserves of rare earth metals far exceed the combined total of the rest of the world.

Metal deposits

▲ Iron	⊗ Lead	▽ Vanadium	⊘ Molybdenum
⋈ Manganese	◁ Tin	▬ Copper	△ Aluminum
△ Nickel	◑ Gold	⊗ Silver	▯ Antimony
Ⓦ Tungsten	⊠ Chromium	◣ Rare earth	⬮ Lithium
⌓ Mercury	▢ Magnesium	◥ Uranium	⊕ Titanium

Nonmetal deposits

◆ Magnesite	◭ Salt mines	■ Coal
△ Sylvite	● Phosphorite	▮ Petroleum
◆ Fluorite	◣ Sulfur	⌂ Natural gas
☾ Mica	▲ Asbestos	
◇ Boron	⣿ Diamond	

Egrets at sunrise

The country also abounds in petroleum, natural gas and oil shale. Petroleum reserves are mainly found in northwest, northeast and north China, as well as in the continental shelves of east China.

Plants and Animals

China is one of the countries with the greatest diversity of wildlife. There are 6,481 species of vertebrates, 10% of the world's total. Among them, 2,404 are terrestrial and 3,862 marine. China boasts more than 32,000 species of higher plants, among which are more than 7,000 species of woody plants (including 2,800 tree species), over 2,000 species of edible plants, and 3,000 species of medicinal plants. Almost all the major plants that grow in the northern hemisphere's frigid, temperate and tropical zones are to be found in China.

Giant panda

Golden monkey, an animal under first-class state protection

Chinese dove-tree, a tree under first-class state protection

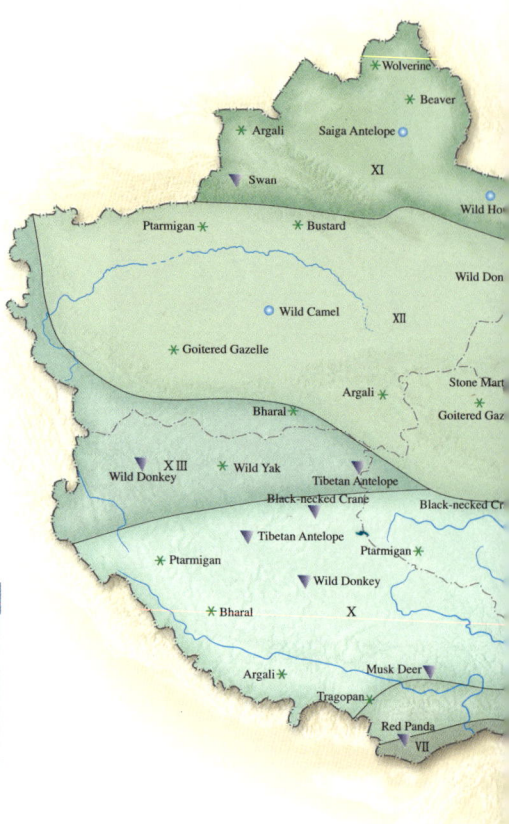

Wolverine
Beaver
Argali
Saiga Antelope
XI
Swan
Wild Hor
Ptarmigan
Bustard
Wild Don
Wild Camel
XII
Goitered Gazelle
Stone Mart
Argali
Bharal
Goitered Gaz
X III
Wild Donkey
Wild Yak
Tibetan Antelope
Black-necked Crane
Black-necked Cr
Tibetan Antelope
Ptarmigan
Ptarmigan
Wild Donkey
Bharal
X
Argali
Musk Deer
Tragopan
Red Panda
VII

Unique Species

There are more than 100 wild animal species unique to China including such well-known rare animals as giant panda, golden monkey, South China tiger, brown-eared pheasant, red-crowned crane, crested ibis, white-flag dolphin and Chinese alligator. The metasequoia, Chinese cypress, Cathay silver fir, China fir, golden larch, Taiwan fir, Fujian cypress, dove-tree, eucommia and camplotheca acuminata are tree species found only in China. The metasequoia, a tall species of arbor, is one of the oldest and rarest plants on earth. The golden larch, one of only five species of rare garden trees in the world, grows in the mountainous areas of the Yangtze River valley. Its coin-shaped leaves on short branches are green in spring and summer, turning yellow in autumn.

I	Zone of cold temperate coniferous forests
II	Zone of mixed temperate coniferous and deciduous broadleaf forests
III	Zone of warm temperate deciduous broadleaf forests
IV	Zone of eastern subtropical evergreen broadleaf forests
V	Zone of western subtropical evergreen broadleaf forests
VI	Zone of eastern tropical rainforests and rainforests
VII	Zone of western tropical rainforests and rainforests
VIII	Zone of temperate grasslands
IX	Zone of warm temperate grasslands
X	Zone of alpine meadow and grasslands
XI	Zone of temperate deserts
XII	Zone of warm temperate deserts
XIII	Zone of alpine deserts

Reindeer

I

Wolverine Moose

Musk Deer

Sable

Swan Northeast China Tiger

Red-crowned Crane

Bustard II

Mandarin Duck

Mongolian Gazelle VIII

Spotted Deer

Bustard Blue Sheep

Mongolian Gazelle Swan

Goitered Gazelle Stoat

Macaque

Long-tailed Pheasant

Brown-eared Pheasant

Giant Salamander III

haral

Argali Macaque Swan

White-lipped Deer White-eared Pheasant Blue Sheep

Golden Monkey Roe Deer

Giant Panda Roe Deer Musk Deer

ask Deer Spotted Deer Spotted Deer White-finned Dolphin

Long-tailed Pheasant Swan Yangtze Crocodile

Tragopan Mandarin Duck

Antelope Tufted Deer White-finned Dolphin Mandarin Duck

V Long-tailed Pheasant

Red Panda Macaque Macaque

den Monkey Golden Monkey Black Muntjac

Giant Salamander Tufted Deer

Tragopan

Crocodile Lizard Taiwan Monkey

Spotted Deer VI

Langur Monkey Black Gibbon Musk Deer

acock VII Long-tailed Pheasant

Wild Elephant VI South China Tiger

Hornbill

Black Gibbon VI

Hainan Eld's Deer

South China Sea Is. inset:

Crocodile Lizard IV Musk Deer

Black Gibbon VI

VI South China Tiger Long-tailed Pheasant

Black Gibbon

Hainan Eld's Deer

VI

South China Sea Is.

○ Animals – hunting totally prohibited by law

▼ Animals – hunting strictly restricted by law

✳ Animals – hunting under State control

Terracotta Warriors and Horses in the
Mausoleum of Qin Shi Huang

History

The Chinese people have created a splendid civilization during a long process of historical evolution, from Da Yu's control of the floods to the "four great inventions," and from the legend of Chang'e flying to the moon to the successful flight of China's first manned spacecraft. While the ancient civilizations of Babylon, Egypt and India fell to invasion or other disasters, Chinese civilization never paused and has developed and continued to this day.

Ancient Civilization

China, one of the world's most ancient civilizations, has a recorded history of nearly 4,000 years. Cultivated rice and millet as well as farming tools have been found in the Hemudu remains in Yuyao, Zhejiang Province, and the Banpo remains near Xi'an in Shaanxi Province. These relics date back 6,000 to 7,000 years. The Chinese mastered the technology of smelting bronze 5,000 years ago. China's earliest dynasty appeared over 4,000 years ago – the Xia Dynasty (2070-1600 BC). During the Shang Dynasty (1600-1046 BC) iron tools came into use. Western Zhou (1046-256 BC) witnessed the emergence of steel production technology. During the Spring and Autumn and the Warring States periods (770-221 BC), there was a great upsurge of intellectual activity, producing many famous philosophers such as Lao Zi, Confucius (Kong Zi), Mencius (Meng Zi), Mo Zi and Han Fei Zi, as well as the well-known military strategist Sun Wu, author of *Art of War*.

Centuries-old painted pot

Unearthed ancient jadeware

Oracle Bone Inscription

In the early 20th century archeologists discovered nearly 100,000 pieces of tortoise shells and cattle bones in the ruins of Yin, capital of the Shang Dynasty, in Anyang, Henan Province. These shells and bones are inscribed with nearly 5,000 different characters, recording various Shang activities, such as worship of ancestors and deities, wars and battles, appointment of officials, construction of cities and fortune telling by divination. The oracle bone inscriptions are the earliest evidence of the Chinese written language discovered so far.

Unification and Dissemination of Civilization

In 221 BC Qin Shi Huang, or the First Emperor of Qin, put an end to the several hundred years of rivalry among independent principalities and established the first centralized, unified, multiethnic feudal state in Chinese history – the Qin

Dynasty (221-206 BC). From then until 1911 China was ruled by altogether 13 unified feudal dynasties and two relatively stable multi-dynasty periods.

During these long years, the "four great inventions" – the compass, papermaking, printing and gunpowder – emerged one after another. Agriculture, handicrafts and commerce flourished, and textile, dyeing, ceramic and smelting technologies were well developed. Around the first year AD, the Han Dynasty (206 BC-AD 220) pioneered the route known as the "Silk Road," from Chang'an (today's Xi'an, Shaanxi Province) through today's Xinjiang and Central Asia, and on to the eastern shores of the Mediterranean. All types of Chinese goods, including silks and porcelains, were traded along the Silk Road. Thereafter, the "four great inventions" and other Chinese advances in science and culture successively spread all over the world.

The Tang Dynasty (618-907) pushed the prosperity of China's feudal society to its peak. By the 660s China's influence had firmly taken root in the Tarim and Junggar basins, and the Ili River valley in the far west, even extended as far as the city-states of Central Asia. During this period, extensive economic and cultural relations were established with many countries, including Japan, Korea, India, Persia and Arabia. Amid a boom in the shipbuilding industry during the Ming Dynasty (1368-1644), Zheng He led a fleet of large ships on seven far-ranging voyages. Visiting some 30 countries, including ones in Southeast Asia and the Maldive Islands, Zheng He's fleet traversed the Indian Ocean and the Persian Gulf, reaching as far as Somalia and Kenya on the eastern coast of Africa.

Bronze horse made in the Eastern Han Dynasty (25-220)

Temple of Heaven, Beijing

Tiananmen Rostrum, Beijing

Post-17th-century Changes

Kangxi (r. 1661-1722), the most renowned emperor of the Qing Dynasty (1644-1911), restored the central empire's rule over Taiwan, and resisted incursions by Tsarist Russia. To reinforce the administration of Tibet, he formulated the rules on the confirmation of the Tibetan local leaders by the Central Government. He effectively administered more than 11 million sq km of Chinese territory. But during the early 19th century the Qing Dynasty declined rapidly. Britain smuggled large quantities of opium into China, leading to the Qing government imposing a ban on the drug. To protect its opium trade, Britain launched a war of aggression against China in 1840, forcing the Qing government to sign the Treaty of Nanjing, a treaty of national betrayal and humiliation. Many countries, including Britain, the US, France, Russia and Japan, coerced the Qing government to sign various unequal treaties, cede territory and pay reparations following the Opium War. China was gradually relegated to the status of a semi-colonial, semi-feudal country.

The Revolution of 1911 led by Dr. Sun Yat-sen was one of the greatest events in modern Chinese history, as it overthrew the Qing Dynasty that had ruled for some 270 years, ended over 2,000 years of feudal monarchy, and founded the Republic of China.

From 1911 to 1949 China was racked by a large number of civil wars. The nation finally won the War of Resistance against Japanese Aggression (1937-1945), the longest counterattack in self-defense in its history.

The People's Republic of China was founded on October 1, 1949. Through 62 years of development, as the party in power, the Communist Party of China has succeeded in bringing about a stable political situation, with economic prosperity, providing ample food and clothing, and active diplomatic engagement, as the world's most populous developing country.

The Path of History

From the founding of the first state in Chinese history to the reform and opening-up era in present-day China, great changes have taken place in this country. Below, we sketch Chinese history chronologically highlighting some key events to discover the country's development path.

● Xia Dynasty (2070 BC-1600 BC)

Xia Dynasty, the First State in Chinese History

The tribal societies of China adopted a power transfer system in which the ruler voluntarily abdicated and selected a worthy man to succeed him in managing tribal affairs. The three famous tribal leaders in the Yellow River region – Yao, Shun and Yu – accomplished power transfer in this way. Upon Yu's death, his son Qi proclaimed himself king, marking the replacement of the old power transfer system by a hereditary system. The first state in Chinese history, the Xia Dynasty, was thus established. It ruled China for over 400 years. In 1600 BC, the Xia Dynasty was overthrown and the Shang Dynasty was set up.

● Shang Dynasty (1600-1046 BC)

● Zhou Dynasty (1046-256 BC)

All Schools of Thought Contending

The period of over 400 years from the seventh to the third centuries BC was the classical era in Chinese philosophy. This epoch witnessed the creation of the main bodies of Chinese philosophy, namely Confucianism, Legalism and Taoism, as well as dozens of other schools of thought, including those of the Military Strategists, Mohism and the Theory of the Five Elements. Confucius and his *Analects*, Lao Zi and his *Classic of the Way and Virtue*, and Sun Wu and his *Art of War* are the most representative of this era.

● Qin Dynasty (221-206 BC)

Qin Dynasty, the First United Empire

In 221 BC Qin Shi Huang (259-210 BC) united China and set up the Qin Dynasty. Qin Shi Huang standardized the written script, weights and measures, and currency, and established the system of prefectures and counties, as well as the system of regulations

and decrees. The feudal governmental structure established by him was subsequently followed for over 2,000 years. The emperor initiated the building of the Great Wall, the thoroughfare leading to the northern grassland and his own huge mausoleum. Such a big empire was difficult to rule, and the Qin Dynasty lasted only 15 years before it was replaced by the Han Dynasty.

● Han Dynasty (206 BC-AD 220)

Zhang Qian's Two Diplomatic Missions to the Western Regions

Emperor Wu (156-87 BC) of the Han Dynasty did much to improve the national strength and extended the Silk Road to the Western Regions (A Han Dynasty term for the area west of the Yumen Pass, including what is now Xinjiang and parts of Central Asia – *tr.*) and even as far as Europe, pushing the Han Empire to its apex. He dispatched Zhang Qian (?-114 BC) as imperial envoy to Dayuezhi, an ancient tribal state in the Western Regions, in 138 BC. In 119 BC Zhang Qian went to the Western Regions for the second time. Zhang's two missions strengthened the contacts between the Han people of the Central Plains and the peoples of Central Asia, and ensured smooth trading activities along the Silk Road.

First General History of China

China's first general history, *Records of the Historian* was completed around 100 BC. The book records Chinese history from the era of the legendary Yellow Emperor to 122 BC, initiating a writing style of presenting history in the form of a series of biographies. The author, Sima Qian (c. 145-87 BC) laid the groundwork for the work of all subsequent historians.

Invention of the Papermaking

In 105 Cai Lun (?-121), a eunuch of the Han Dynasty, invented a technique of making paper from tree bark, fishnets, rags and hemp. Such paper was well suited for writing, and its raw materials were cheap and easily come by, facilitating the spread of writing in China and around the world.

- Three Kingdoms Period (220-280)
- Jin Dynasty (265-420)
- Northern & Southern Dynasties (420-589)
- Sui Dynasty (581-618)

Grand Canal

After the Han Dynasty, China was ruled successively by the Three Kingdoms, Jin Dynasty and Northern & Southern Dynasties. This was a period of constant division. It was the Sui Dynasty that united China again.

Yang Guang (569-618), the second Sui emperor, was an eccentric and domineering character. Before ascending the throne he brought false charges against the empress and the crown prince, and in 604 killed his own father to establish himself as the next emperor. After taking the throne, he lived an extremely extravagant and luxurious life, and drafted millions of peasants to build a canal linking the northern and southern parts of China, in order to make it easier for him to tour the lower reaches of the Yangtze River. Then he drafted soldiers for three successive years to attack the Koryo Kingdom on the Korean Peninsula. Moreover, despite dwindling national financial resources, he had Luoyang built as the eastern capital. All this threw the country into turbulence, with frequent peasant uprisings. In the end, he was assassinated by his generals, and the Sui Dynasty collapsed.

- Tang Dynasty (618-907)

Princess Wencheng in Tibet

The Sui Dynasty was succeeded by that of the Tang. In 641 Emperor Taizong sent his daughter Princess Wencheng (625-680) to marry Songtsam Gambo (?-650), King of Tubo (now Tibet). During her 40 years in Tibet, showing extraordinary political genius, she assisted Songtsam Gambo in governing Tubo and preserving peace between the Tang Dynasty and that kingdom, thus winning the respect of the Tibetan people. When she first arrived in Tibet, she brought many scholars, musicians and agricultural technicians with her, as well as large quantities of tools. Later, she introduced the techniques of rearing silkworms, and making wine and paper to Tibet. As a result, both cultural and economic development advanced rapidly in the region.

Jianzhen in Japan

Jianzhen (688-763), an eminent monk of the Tang Dynasty, at the age of 14 was initiated into the Lü (Vinaya) sect of Buddhism. In the year 753 he was invited by a Japanese monastery to preach there. He took with him advanced Chinese knowledge of architecture, sculpture, painting and medicine.

● Song Dynasty (960-1279)

Invention of Movable-type Printing

The Song Dynasty was another era when China was united again after the Tang Dynasty. It lasted over 30 years under the reign of 16 emperors. During this dynasty, handcrafts developed rapidly, while remarkable technical innovations were made in the fields of mining and metallurgy, textiles, porcelain making, shipbuilding, and papermaking. Bi Sheng (?-c. 1051) invented movable-type printing. He carved individual characters on clay cubes and heated them into pottery. The pottery types were arranged within an iron frame. Printing and typesetting could proceed at the same time, and the pottery types could be reused repeatedly. Movable-type printing is considered a major revolution in the printing history of humankind.

● Yuan Dynasty (1271-1368)
● Ming Dynasty (1368-1644)

Zheng He's Seven Voyages

The Yuan Dynasty was the first united feudal dynasty ruled by a non-Han people in the history of China. In 1368 Zhu Yuanzhang, a leader of the Red Turban rebels, overthrew the Yuan Dynasty and established the Ming Dynasty. In the space of two centuries the Ming made great achievements in economy, culture, science and technology. Not long after the dynasty was established, Zheng He (1371-1435), a eunuch, was assigned by the central authorities to lead huge fleets to explore the Western Seas on seven voyages from 1405 to 1433. They passed through 30 countries and reached as far as the east coast of Africa and the Red Sea estuary. The voyages promoted economic exchanges between China and other Asian countries, and Africa.

Recapture of Taiwan by Zheng Chenggong

The Qing Dynasty was the last feudal regime. In 1616 the Manchu people in north China set up the Qing Dynasty, and in 1644 entered the Central Plains through the Shanhai Pass, and replaced the Ming Dynasty. Zheng Chenggong (1624-1662), a Ming Dynasty general, organized a big fleet in southeastern China and resisted the Qing conquest until 1662, when he retreated to Taiwan with over 20,000 men and several hundred ships.

In the early 17th century the Dutch East India Company invaded Taiwan and made it a trading colony. In 1662 Zheng Chenggong fought the Dutch troops and recaptured Taiwan and the Penghu Islands (called Pescadores by the Portuguese), establishing Chinese sovereignty there. In 1684 the Qing government set up, under its direct control, Taiwan Prefecture, and later Taiwan Province.

Establishment of Dalai and Panchen Titles

In 1653 Qing Emperor Shunzhi officially confirmed the title of Dalai Lama on the Fifth Dalai. In 1713 Qing Emperor Kangxi dispatched an envoy to confirm the title of Panchen Erdini on the Fifth Panchen. The Qing court also stipulated that the Dalai and Panchen lamas of later generations must be authorized by the Central Government. This system has been maintained to the present day.

First Opium War

Britain forced China to open its doors by smuggling opium into China in the early 19th century. Chinese official Lin Zexu burned nearly 1.2 million kg of opium in public at Humen, Guangdong, in 1839. On June 28, 1840 a British naval fleet blocked the mouth of the Pearl River, seized Xiamen, Shanghai and other ports, and sailed up the Yangtze River to attack Nanjing.

Treaty of Nanking

On August 29, 1842, when British troops arrived at the city walls of Nanjing, the Qing government was forced to sign the unequal Treaty of Nanking. According to the Treaty, China had to cede Hong Kong to Britain and open up five treaty ports, as well as pay huge sums in reparations. The US, France, Spain and Italy, in succession, obtained the same privileges by force. China was hence relegated to being a semi-colony of the Western powers.

Second Opium War

From 1856 to 1860 the British and French allied fleet, supported by Russia and the US, launched the Second Opium War on China and forced the Qing government to sign more unequal treaties with the four countries. Apart from enormous amounts in reparations, China lost large areas of territory. The Yuanmingyuan (Garden of Perfection and Brightness), known as the "garden of gardens," in Beijing was destroyed by the British and French allied forces.

Westernization Movement

The Westernization Movement, which thrived from the 1860s to the mid-1890s, was initiated by the Qing government to learn from Western capitalist countries in respect of military, political, economic, cultural and diplomatic techniques. Its activities included setting up military industry and related enterprises, equipping the army and navy with new-type weapons, and dispatching Chinese students to study in Europe and North America. The Movement was intended to make China strong and prosperous, but ended in failure.

Sino-French War

In 1883 French colonists provoked a war on the border of China and Vietnam. In the following year French troops attacked Qing troops in Lang Son in Vietnam and the Chinese fleets in Taiwan and Fujian. The Sino-French War unfolded in Taiwan and Vietnam at the same time. During the war the French troops were defeated, and consequently the French cabinet fell from power. The Qing government could have won a victory, but it signed a truce agreement with France in 1885 – the Treaty of Tientsin. China lost an important fleet in the southeast coast, while France was able to infiltrate China's Yunnan, Guangxi and Kwangchowan.

Sino-Japanese War 1894-1895

In 1894 Japan invaded Korea and China, and Chinese soldiers and civilians fought back, resulting in the First Sino-Japanese War. Soon the Japanese troops controlled the Korean Peninsula, took command of the sea after battles in the Yellow Sea, and then attacked China's northeastern cities and coastal cities in Shandong, defeated China's Beiyang Fleet. In 1895 the two sides signed the Treaty of Shimonoseki, which imposed heavy debts on the Chinese government and reduced China further to a semi-colonial and semi-feudal society.

Reform Movement

In 1898 Kang Youwei (1858-1927), together with others, started a reform movement involving political, military, economic and cultural changes. They dreamed of establishing a constitutional monarchy in China with the support of the Qing government, to make the country strong and prosperous. The movement encountered stiff resistance from royal conservatives and, after lasting 100 days, was ended by a cruel massacre.

● Republic of China (1912-1949)

Revolution of 1911

The Revolution of 1911 was a democratic revolution led by Sun Yat-sen. In 1911, when the Qing government planned to give the authority for railway construction in China to foreign companies, forces from all quarters united to rise up and seize political power in the southern prov-

inces. On January 1, 1912 the provisional government of the Republic of China was founded in Nanjing. On February 12 the last Qing emperor was forced to abdicate, and the 2,000-year feudal monarchy was replaced with a republic.

May 4th Movement

The May 4th Movement of 1919 is regarded as the ideological origin of many important events in modern Chinese history. Its direct cause was the unequal treaties imposed on China after World War I. Motivated by strong patriotism, students initiated the movement, which further developed into a national protest movement involving people from all sectors of society. It also marked the introduction to China of various new ideologies, among which the spread of Marxism-Leninism is especially noteworthy.

Birth of the CPC

In 1921 a body of 13 delegates, including Mao Zedong (1893-1976), representing communist groups throughout the country, held the First National Congress in Shanghai to found the Communist Party of China (CPC). Today's CPC, with over 80 million members, is the mainstay of Chinese society. Mao Zedong, one of the founders of the CPC and the People's Republic of China, made extraordinary contributions to China's revolution and construction. He was a revolutionary and militarist, as well as a poet and calligrapher.

War of Resistance against Japanese Aggression

From 1937 to 1945 the Chinese people struggled doggedly against the aggression of Japanese imperialism, and won the final victory in what is known as the War of Resistance against Japanese Aggression. Chinese military and civilian casualties exceeded 35 million; and China's direct economic losses, from 1937 figures converted to current value, surpassed US$100 billion, with indirect losses of over US$500 billion, as well as the loss of incalculably precious cultural heritage items.

● People's Republic of China (1949-   )

Founding of the People's Republic

On October 1, 1949 a grand ceremony witnessed by crowds of people was held on the Tiananmen Square in Beijing. At the ceremony Mao Zedong, chairman of the Central People's Government, solemnly proclaimed the founding of the People's Republic of China.

First Five-year Plan

The First Five-year Plan (1953-1957) accomplished great achievements: the average annual increase rate of national income reached 8.9% or higher; a number of basic industries necessary for national industrialization, until then non-existent domestically, were established, including ones for producing airplanes, automobiles, heavy and precision machinery, power-generating equipment, metallurgical and mining equipment, high-grade alloy steels and non-ferrous metals.

From that time on, the Chinese government set economic objectives for every five years. The 12th Five-year Plan (2011-2015) is now under way.

Reform and Opening Up

The Third Plenary Session of the 11th CPC Central Committee, held at the end of 1978, ushered in a new historic era for China. Chinese leader Deng Xiaoping (1904-1997) vigorously promoted the policy of reform and opening up, and placed the national work focus on modernization. A road to modernization with Chinese characteristics was gradually established, through opening up and reforms in the economic, political and cultural systems. In 1992 Deng Xiaoping, the principal architect of China's reform and opening up, during a southern inspection tour made some important speeches, collectively regarded as key endorsement for economic reform and social progress in the following years.

Jiang Zemin and Hu Jintao became General Secretary of the CPC Central Committee in 1989 and in 2002, respectively. They inherited and developed the policy of reform and opening up initiated by Deng Xiaoping, and respectively put forth the important thought of Three Represents and the Scientific Outlook on Development, with the result that China has attained rapid economic growth and remarkable improvement of people's lives, attracting world attention.

Return of Hong Kong and Macao to China

China resumed its sovereignty over Hong Kong on July 1, 1997, and over Macao on December 20, 1999, establishing Hong Kong Special Administrative Region (HKSAR) and Macao Special Administrative Region (MSAR), respectively. The Central Government applies the basic policies of "one country, two systems" and "a high degree of autonomy" to the two places. "One country, two systems" refers to the fact that in China, a unified country, the mainland practices the socialist system, while Hong Kong and Macao retain their original capitalist system and way of life unchanged for 50 years.

Morning in Shenzhen

Administrative Divisions / Beijing / Shanghai / Tianjin / Chongqing /
Hong Kong Special Administrative Region / Macao Special Administrative Region /
Taiwan / Urbanization Process

Administrative Divisions and Cities

China is divided into 23 provinces, five autonomous regions, four municipalities
directly under the Central Government and two special administrative regions.
Since the policy of reform and opening up was introduced in 1978, the country's
rapid economic development has brought about an accelerating process of urbanization. China's achievements in developing cities have drawn the world's attention.
However, new problems are arising. A serious question for China in the 21st century is how to promote the urbanization process in a positive and stable way.

Administrative Divisions

The whole country is divided into provinces, autonomous regions and municipalities directly under the Central Government. A province or an autonomous region is further subdivided into cities with districts, autonomous prefectures, counties and autonomous counties. Counties and autonomous counties are subdivided into townships, ethnic townships and towns.

Municipalities directly under the Central Government and large cities are subdivided into districts, counties and cities without districts. Autonomous prefectures are subdivided into counties, autonomous counties and cities without districts. Autonomous regions, autonomous prefectures and autonomous counties are all autonomous ethnic-minority areas.

The state establishes special administrative regions when necessary. The system implemented in special administrative regions will be stipulated by law, as set by the NPC and depending on actual conditions.

At present, there are 23 provinces, five autonomous regions, four municipalities directly under the Central Government and two special administrative regions.

Legend

★	Capital
⊙	Provincial-level administrative centers
	National border
	Undefined national border
	Boundary lines of provinces, autonomous regions and municipalities
	Boundary lines of special administrative regions

Proportion of Provinces, Autonomous Regions and Municipalities in National Territory Areas

Province
Municipality
Autonomous region
Special administrative region

Heilong River

Heilongjiang Province

⊙Harbin

⊙Changchun
Jilin Province

Shenyang

Inner Mongolia Autonomous Region

Liaoning Province

Hohhot

Hebei Province

Beijing
Beijing Municipality ★ ⊙Tianjin
Tianjin Municipality

Bohai Sea

Gansu Province

Yellow River

Yinchuan

Taiyuan

Shijiazhuang

Ningxia Hui Autonomous Region

Qinghai Province   Xining

Shanxi Province

Lanzhou

Jinan

Shandong Province

Yellow Sea

Shaanxi Province

Yellow River

Zhengzhou

Jiangsu Province

Xi'an

Henan Province

Anhui Province

Nanjing

Shanghai Municipality
Shanghai

Sichuan Province

Hubei Province

Hefei

Yangtze River

Chengdu⊙

Wuhan

Jiangtze River

Hangzhou

Chongqing Chongqing Municipality

Changsha⊙

Zhejiang Province

East China Sea

Nanchang

Jiangxi Province

Guizhou Province

Hunan Province

Chiwei Island

Lancang River

⊙Guiyang

Fuzhou

Diaoyu Island

Kunming

Fujian Province

Taibei

Taiwan Straits

Yunnan Province

Guangxi Zhuang Autonomous Region

Guangdong Province

Taiwan

Taiwan Island

⊙Nanning

Guangzhou

Penghu Islands

Pearl River

Hong Kong
Macao   Hong Kong SAR
Macao SAR

Dongsha Islands

⊙Haikou

South China Sea

Hainan Province
Hainan Island

Beijing

Beijing is the capital of China. Boasting a history of over 3,000 years as a city and over 850 years as a capital, Beijing is the political, transportation and cultural center of China, as well as the host city of the 29th Olympic Games in 2008.

Hall of Prayer for Good Harvests in the Temple of Heaven

Beijing was the capital of six feudal dynasties, leaving it a legacy of a great number of imperial buildings, as well as ancient gardens, temples and tombs. Among these buildings, the Imperial Palace is the largest palace complex in the world; the Temple of Heaven is the largest heaven-worshipping complex in ancient China; the Summer Palace is the most famous imperial garden in China; the Ming Tombs is the largest imperial mausoleum group in China...

Typical of Beijing's traditional residences is *siheyuan*, which is composed of the main house facing south, the opposite house facing north, side houses which adjoin the main house and

The World Trade Center in Beijing's Central Business District

face east and west, and a courtyard in the center. The *siheyuan* is usually built with grey tiles and bricks. The narrow lanes between *siheyuan* are called *hutong*. Beijing is the municipality with the most UNESCO World Heritage sites in the world.

Beijing is the most important center of finance and business in China. Many multinationals have set up their China headquarters in Beijing. Among the world's top 500 corporations in 2010, 30 were headquartered in Beijing, which ranks second in the world in terms of the number of top 500 corporations represented. Beijing is the only inland city in China chosen among the "world's 15 cities for shopping" for its over 100 large and medium-sized shopping malls. Wangfujing, Qianmen and Xidan are traditional business districts, while the China World Mall, and the malls at Oriental Plaza and Zhongguancun Plaza are new shopping venues that have risen in recent years.

The Beijing municipal government has set the goal to build the city into a hub of the world's economic system and the world's city network by 2020.

Shanghai

Shanghai is the largest city on China's mainland, and an important center of economy, finance, trade and shipping. It was the host city of the 41st World Expo in 2010.

Shanghai has China's largest foreign trade port and largest industrial base. It ranks first among Chinese mainland cities in economic aggregate, per capita GDP and per capita disposable income.

The "Shanghai-style culture" has developed from traditional culture in the regions south of the Yangtze River and integrated with European and American cultures since it was opened as a trading port. This culture is ancient and modern, traditional and fashionable at the same time.

As an international metropolis, Shanghai has numerous high-rises that symbolize its prosperity. It also has historic sites such as the ancient town of Fengjing. The Bund and the *shikumen* alleys at Tianzifang represent typical Shanghai architecture, which combines both Western and Eastern elements. On the Bund in Puxi a row of buildings in the classical style of Western Europe form a splendid international architecture exhibition.

With its modern culture and numerous historic sites, Shanghai attracts Chinese and foreign tourists alike. It is the largest destination in China for overseas tourists and the largest home port and destination for luxury cruises. Luxury cruise tourism in Shanghai makes up over 70% of China's total business in this sector.

Shanghai is working to build the city into an international financial and world shipping center by 2020.

Shikumen house, Shanghai

Shanghai

Tianjin's Xingang Port

Tianjin

Tianjin is the economic center of north China, an international port city and an ecological city. Located in the center of the Bohai Economic Rim, it is the birthplace of China's modern industry, and one of the coastal cities in north China that were opened to the world in modern times. Over 600 years, particularly the past 100 years, Tianjin has developed into a unique city with both Western and Eastern elements and ancient and modern styles. One can get to know the 100-year modern history of China by visiting Tianjin.

With the fourth largest industrial base and the third largest foreign trade port in China, Tianjin has regained its momentum of rapid development since 2006 when the Binhai New Area was included in national preferential policies. Tianjin will host the Sixth East Asian Games in 2013.

Chongqing

Located in southwest China, Chongqing is one of the four municipalities directly under the Central Government and one of the five key cities on China's mainland, the economic and financial center of the upper reaches of the Yangtze River, and a pilot area where the state carries out coordinated reform for balanced urban and

Chongqing

rural development. Chongqing is home to the state-level Liangjiang New Area.

Chongqing was the wartime capital of China during the War of Resistance against Japanese Aggression (1937-1945), thus it has a unique culture dating from that period. For its numerous mountains and misty climate, it is also known as a "city of fog" and a "mountain city." Within Chongqing there are two World Heritage sites, and the nearby Three Gorges is the most famous natural scenery in China. Hotpot is the typical food of Chongqing.

In recent years Chongqing has developed rapidly, and become a key city in western China. Chongqing is a historically and culturally famous city, an important base of modern manufacturing, and a transport hub in southwest China. The municipal government is endeavoring to build the city into a "livable city" with smooth traffic and more forest coverage enhancing the quality of life.

Key Cities of China

The "key cities of China" are those that have a broad impact on a large area in the political, economic and cultural sectors, and act as an economic powerhouse over the surrounding areas. In February 2010 the Ministry of Housing and Urban-Rural Construction issued the National Urban System Plan (Draft), which states that five key cities will be built up: Beijing and Tianjin in the Bohai Economic Rim, Shanghai in east China, Guangzhou in south China, and Chongqing in southwest China.

Hong Kong Special Administrative Region

The Hong Kong Special Administrative Region (HKSAR) is located on the east of the estuary of the Pearl River. It covers an area of 1,104 sq km, and has a population of over seven million.

Hong Kong was occupied by Britain after the Opium War of 1840. In accordance with the Sino-British Joint Declaration on the Question of Hong Kong, signed in 1984, China resumed its exercise of sovereignty over Hong Kong on July 1, 1997, when the HKSAR was formally established. The Chinese government has carried out the basic policies of "one country, two systems," "administration of Hong Kong by the Hong Kong people," and "a high degree of autonomy" in Hong Kong. "One country, two systems" refers to the fact that in China, a unified country, the mainland practices the socialist system, while Hong Kong retains its original capitalist system and way of life unchanged for 50 years; "administration of Hong Kong by the Hong Kong people" means that the HKSAR is administered by the Hong Kong people alone, who enjoy "a high degree of autonomy." The HKSAR fully enjoys autonomous administrative, legislative, independent judicial and final adjudication powers. The present Chief Executive of the HKSAR is Donald Tsang Yam-kuen. The HKSAR's regional flag features a blossoming bauhinia, a local flower.

Hong Kong is a free port, which does not levy customs tariffs on imports except for four dutiable commodities: tobacco, alcoholic beverages, hydrocarbon oil and

Night view of Hong Kong

methyl alcohol. It ranks 11th in the global trade and economic system, 6th among the foreign exchange markets, and 15th among banking centers. Its stock market is the third largest in Asia. Hong Kong is also a major exporter of ready-made clothing, clocks and watches, toys, games, electronics, and some light industry products, and its total export value ranks among the top ones in the world. China's mainland is the main trading partner for Hong Kong, as well as the main provider of its drinking water, vegetables, meat, poultry and eggs.

Macao Special Administrative Region

The Macao Special Administrative Region (MSAR) is located on the west of the estuary of the Pearl River. Over 500,000 people live on a land area of 32.8 sq km, making Macao one of the most densely populous regions in the world.

Macao was occupied by Portugal as long ago as in the 16th century. In

Façade of St. Paul's Cathedral, Macao

accordance with the Sino-Portugal Joint Declaration on the Question of Macao, signed in 1987, China resumed its exercise of sovereignty over Macao on December 20, 1999, when the MSAR was formally established. The Chinese government has carried out the basic policies of "one country, two systems," "administration of Macao by the Macao people," and "a high degree of autonomy" in Macao. "One country, two systems" refers to the fact that in China, a unified country, the mainland practices the socialist system, while Macao retains its original capitalist system and way of life unchanged for 50 years; "administration of Macao by the Macao people" means that the MSAR is administered by the Macao people alone, who enjoy "a high degree of autonomy." The MSAR fully enjoys autonomous administrative and legislative, and independent judicial and final adjudication powers. The present Chief Executive of the MSAR is Fernando Chui Sai On. The design of the MSAR's regional flag is a lotus flower in bloom.

The integration and co-existence of Western and Eastern cultures makes Macao a special city with both traditional Chinese temples and grand Catholic churches, plus many historic and cultural legacies and a beautiful coastal landscape.

As one of the two international free trade ports in China, Macao enjoys full FIO rights in cargo, capital, foreign currencies and personnel. Known as the Monte Carlo of the East, Macao boasts thriving tourism and gaming industries, which are the most important economic engines of this city.

Taiwan

Taiwan is the largest island in China. Located by the southeast coastal continental shelf of China's mainland, the Taiwan region consists of Taiwan Island and its affiliated islands, Penghu Islands, and the islands of Jinmen, Mazu and others, covering a land area of about 36,000 sq km. Taiwan has a population of 23 million, with 98% being from the Han group. The major dialects are Hokkien and Hakka. Most Taiwan residents believe in Confucianism, Buddhism and Taoism, which were taken to Taiwan by migrants from the mainland's Fujian and Guangdong provinces. Taiwan has well-developed industry and commerce. Its economy is export-oriented, and its information and semiconductor industries take the lead in the world. Taiwan was once one of the "Four Asian Tigers."

Since ancient times Taiwan has been an inalienable part of the sacred territory of China. As early as the Song Dynasty (960-1279) the Chinese government had exercised effective jurisdiction over Taiwan. After its defeat in the Sino-Japanese War of 1894-1895 the Qing government was forced to cede Taiwan to Japan. Japan then occupied Taiwan for the next 50 years. In October 1945 Taiwan was recovered after the Chinese nation, including Taiwan compatriots, fought dauntlessly and won the War of Resistance against Japanese Aggression. In 1949 the Kuomintang authorities lost the civil war with the CPC and retreated to Taiwan, in confrontation with China's mainland and with support from the US. Thus was created the issue of Taiwan.

Although reunification has not been realized, the reality of Taiwan as an inseparable part of China's territory has never changed and has been recognized by

Taipei 101, the world's second tallest building

Mainland tourists dancing with the local people of Mount Ali, Taiwan

Commercial Exchanges and People-to-People Contacts

With the improvement of cross-Straits relations, economic and trade contacts have also been growing, and people-to-people exchanges and cooperation in different fields have been deepening. In 2010 the total trade volume across the Straits reached US$145.37 billion-worth, up 36.9% year on year. There were 5.14 million visits by Taiwan residents to the mainland, up 14.6%; and the visits of mainland residents to Taiwan came to 1.66 million, up 77.6%, including 1.228 million visits for tourism, an increase of 92.7%. By the end of 2010 the ARATS and the SET had signed 15 agreements and reached two common understandings. Over 83,000 businesses had been set up on the mainland with a total of US$52 billion of Taiwanese investment.

international organizations including the UN and most countries. It is a common wish and sacred mission of the Chinese nation, including the Taiwan compatriots, to resolve the issue of Taiwan and realize the reunification of the country as soon as possible.

Over the last 60 years, the CPC and the Chinese government have made unremitting efforts to resolve the issue of Taiwan and realize the reunification of the country, and worked hard to improve and develop the relations between the two sides across the Taiwan Straits. Mao Zedong, Zhou Enlai and others of the first generation of the central leadership raised the idea of seeking a peaceful solution to the issue of Taiwan. On January 1, 1979 the NPC Standing Committee published the "Message to Compatriots in Taiwan," declaring that the Central Government would work hard to realize the peaceful reunification of the country, and advocating that direct links of mail, transportation and trade be resumed, and people-to-people contacts and bilateral exchanges be promoted. Deng Xiaoping proposed the idea of "one country, two systems," making historic contributions to the establishment of the policy of "peaceful reunification and one country, two systems." In 1995 Jiang Zemin put forward eight proposals for developing relations between the two sides and promoting the peaceful reunification of the country, which helped improve cross-Straits relations.

In March 2005 the Third Session of the 10th NPC adopted the Anti-Secession Law with an overwhelming majority in favor, demonstrating the Chinese people's common will and determination to oppose "Taiwan independence" and safeguard China's sovereignty and territorial integrity. In April, at the invitation of General Secretary Hu Jintao of the CPC Central Committee, Lien Chan, chairman of the Chinese Kuomintang, visited the mainland with a delegation. Top leaders of the CPC and the Kuomintang then held their first meeting in 60 years since the Kuomintang retreated to Taiwan, and issued the "Common Aspiration and Prospects for Peaceful Cross-Straits Development," establishing common political ground for opposing "Taiwan independence" and adhering to the "1992 Consensus." In 2007, at the 17th CPC National Congress, General Secretary Hu Jintao stated that the compatriots on both sides needed to work together to firmly oppose and contain secessionist activities for "Taiwan independence" and keep to the theme of peaceful development of cross-Straits relations.

In March 2008 Ma Ying-jeou was elected local leader of Taiwan, and took power as leader of the Kuomintang. The situation in Taiwan has since then experienced positive changes, and cross-Straits relations have welcomed this historic opportunity. In May 2008 Hu Jintao met with Wu Po-hsiung, chairman of the Kuomintang, and stressed that the CPC and the Kuomintang and the people on both sides of the Taiwan Straits must work together to establish mutual trust, put aside disputes, seek common ground while reserving differences for a mutually beneficial situation, continue following and implementing the "Common Aspiration and Prospects for Peaceful Cross-Straits Development," and make practical progress in promoting cross-Straits relations. On December 31, at a forum commemorating the 30th anniversary of the publication of the "Message to Compatriots in Taiwan,"

Hu Jintao delivered a speech titled, "Join Hands to Promote the Peaceful Development of Cross-Straits Relations and Achieve the Great Rejuvenation of the Chinese Nation," explaining in a comprehensive and systematic way the important idea of peaceful development of cross-Straits relations. The speech thus became a programmatic document for guiding the work on Taiwan in the new circumstances.

In recent years the two sides of the Taiwan Straits have intensified exchanges and cooperation for common development. In June 2008, on the basis of the "1992 Consensus," the Association for Relations across the Taiwan Strait (ARATS) and the Straits Exchanges Foundation (SET) restored talks in Beijing, reviving institutionalized negotiations across the Straits after a nine-year hiatus. The two sides signed a memorandum on charter flights across the Straits and an agreement on mainland residents traveling to Taiwan. In July the mainland residents were officially allowed by the Taiwan authorities to visit Taiwan for tourism. In December the direct, bilateral links of mail, transport and trade that compatriots across the Straits had long awaited were finally realized.

In May 2010 the 41st World Expo was held in Shanghai, and Taiwan participated 40 years after its previous participation. In June the ARATS and the SET signed the Economic Cooperation Framework Agreement (ECFA) and an agreement on intellectual property rights protection. It was an important milestone in the history of cross-Straits relations. In November Taiwan sent a delegation to take part in the 16th Asian Games in Guangzhou, and reached seventh place. Also in 2010 the Taiwan authorities declared that they would recognize the qualifications awarded by 41 top universities on the mainland, while the mainland declared that Taiwanese high school graduates who scored within the top 12% on the General Scholastic Ability Test could apply for admission to 123 mainland universities, marking a breakthrough by the two sides in recognizing higher education certificates.

Urbanization Process

Since the policy of reform and opening up was introduced in 1978 China's economy has developed rapidly. As a result, the urbanization process has accelerated. China has over 660 cities at present. Over the decades, great changes have taken place in every city:

Beijing's politics, culture and economy are developing in a balanced way; the ancient city of Xi'an integrates history and fashion; Shanghai displays its splendor as an international metropolis; and the Shenzhen Special Economic Zone is developing rapidly....

It's predicted that in this century 10 major conurbations will form in the coastal areas, the hinterland and border areas, and become the best regions for potential development. Among them, the Beijing-Tianjin-Hebei Region, the Yangtze River Delta and the Pearl River Delta had already become China's leading economic regions by the end of the 20th century, and are expected to continue taking the lead in the future. During the 12th Five-year Plan period (2011-2015) China will enter a new phase, when urbanization and urban development will both experience a transformation; the urbanization level will increase by 0.8 to 1.0 percentage point every year and reach 65% by 2030. A major task that China faces is to push forward the urbanization process in a positive and prudent way.

Qingdao

In the face of highly accelerated urbanization, the Central Government has tried to coordinate population, land, environment, and economic and social development by making strategic regional plans while working hard to keep urbanization an orderly process. In the course of city planning, China implements "strict control over the size of large cities, rational development of medium-sized cities, and active development of small cities." Medium-sized cities with populations of between 200,000 and 500,000 and small cities with populations fewer than 200,000 have grown rapidly since the 1980s, while large cities with populations of over one million have developed satellite cities and towns in a planned way.

The expansion of cities and the rapid growth of urban population have resulted in such problems as high intensity downtown areas, heavy traffic, worsening environmental quality, high land prices and rents, and rising unemployment. The cities are developing on a bigger scale, pay-

Satellite Towns

The planning of satellite towns is linked to the urbanization process. Satellite towns play an irreplaceable role in solving problems caused by the excessive expansion of big cities. Similar to those in other countries, satellite towns in China are built for two main purposes: One is to decentralize population, industry or scientific and research institutes from the big cities, and the other is to develop new industries, particularly tertiary industries, on the periphery of big cities.

In planning satellite towns China has worked toward the goals of relatively bigger populations, multiple functions, balance between land for work and land for residence, and convenient transportation systems with the parent city. The low-carbon principle is followed in building the satellite towns, to achieve balanced development between the parent city and its satellite town (towns) and between satellite towns themselves.

Migrant workers, an important force in China's urban construction

Public bicycle rental is a part of "green travel."

ing more attention to improving the living conditions of migrant workers and building a green urban environment. According to experts' analysis, second- and third-tier cities will become the new destinations of migrant workers and university graduates, and thus lessening the employment pressure on major cities. The digital urban management has been spread to many cities so far, and will be spread across the country on the basis of an improved technical platform.

To readjust the urban-rural structure and regional structures, and to realize sustained, stable and relatively rapid economic development, China needs to balance the development of big, medium-sized and small cities. It is predicted that the regional economies will develop into a grid, with urban regional economies including the Harbin-Changchun Economic Zone, Bohai Economic Rim, Central Shaanxi Plain, Yangtze River Delta, Central China, Chengdu-Chongqing, Pearl River Delta, Cross-Straits Economic Zone and Beibu Gulf Economic Zone. Conurbations will become important supports for China's economic development in the future.

Temple fair to celebrate the
Lantern Festival

Population and Ethnicity

China has the world's largest population, with 56 ethnic groups enjoying harmonious coexistence. They live together over vast areas, with some living in compact communities in small areas. *Hanyu* (Chinese language) is the most commonly used language in China, while most of the 55 minority peoples have their own languages. China's major traditional festivals include Spring Festival, Lantern Festival, Qingming Festival, Dragon-boat Festival, and Mid-autumn Festival. The ethnic minorities also celebrate their own traditional festivals. A large number of religions coexist in China.

Population

China is the most populous country in the world, with 1.339 billion people (the 6th national census in 2010) or about one-fifth of the world's total population.

It has a high population density, with 140 people per sq km. This population, however, is unevenly distributed. The eastern coastal areas are densely populated, with more than 400 people per sq km; in the central areas this figure is over 200; while in the sparsely populated plateaus in the west there are fewer than 10 people per sq km.

Population Increment

When the People's Republic of China was founded in 1949, the population numbered 541.67 million. Following that, owing to China's stable society, rapid development of production, improvement in medical and health care conditions, insufficient awareness of the importance of population growth control, as well as shortage of experience, the population grew rapidly, reaching 806.71 million in 1969. Since the 1970s China has implemented a policy of family planning to control population growth. Now, its population reproduction picture has basically been turned around, into one characterized by low rates of birth, death and increase.

The Chinese government adheres to the policy of tackling population and development in a unified way, and has integrated population development into the overall plan for national economic and social development, striving for

Sketch Map Showing Distribution of Population Density

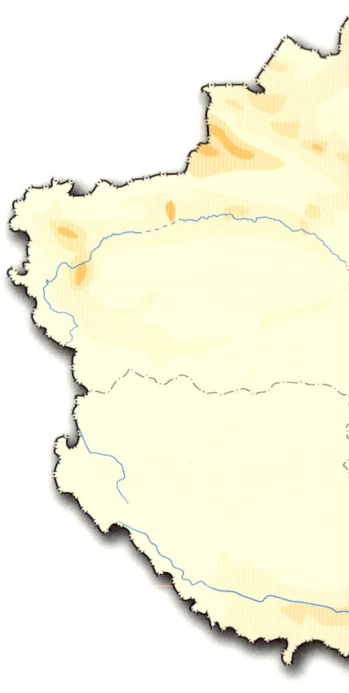

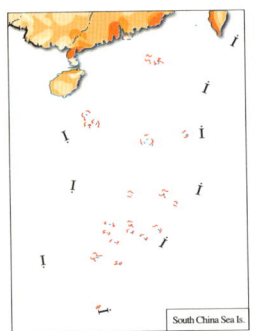

South China Sea Is.

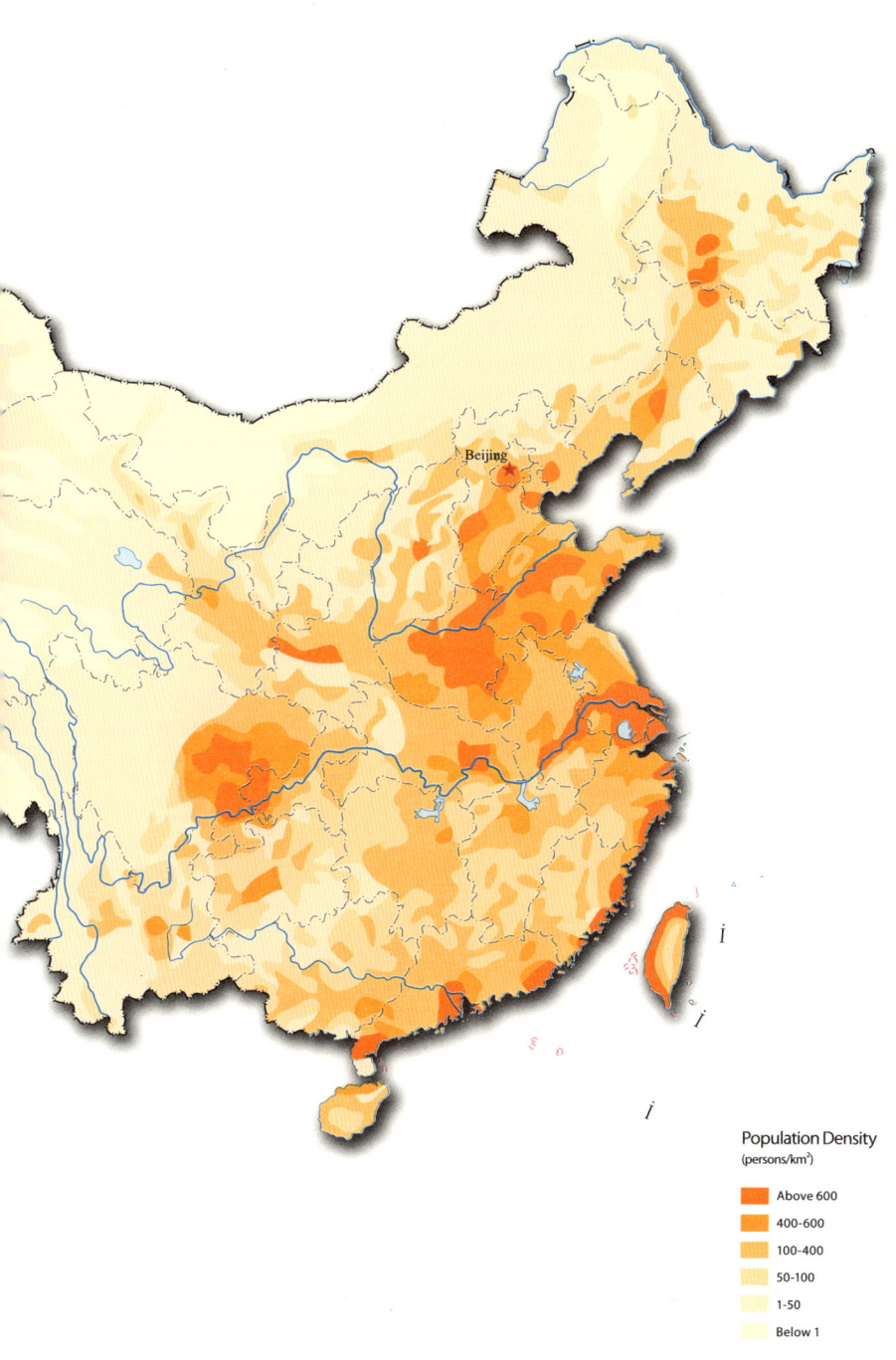

Beijing

Population Density
(persons/km²)

▮	Above 600
▮	400-600
▮	100-400
▮	50-100
▮	1-50
▮	Below 1

Family Planning

Family planning is one of China's basic state policies, combining government guidance with voluntary compliance by citizens. The central and local governments have instituted policies and regulations for controlling population growth, and improving population quality and structure, as well as macro plans on population development. Governments also provide consultation, guidance and technical services concerning reproductive care, contraception, healthy births and child-rearing. Couples of child-bearing age, guided by relevant state policies and regulations, can make arrangements for pregnancy and childbirth in an appropriate and responsible manner, and choose appropriate contraceptive methods, taking their age, health, employment and financial situations into consideration.

The basic requirements for family planning: late marriage and late child-bearing, having fewer but healthier babies, especially one child per couple. But a flexible practice is adopted for rural people and ethnic minorities. In rural areas couples may have a second baby in exceptional cases, but must wait several years after the birth of the first child. In areas inhabited by minority peoples, each community may work out its own regulations in accordance with its wishes, population, natural resources, economy, culture and customs; in general, such couples may have a second baby, or a third in some places. As for ethnic minorities with extremely small populations, couples may have as many children as they wish.

balanced population and socio-economic development, and resources utilization compatible with environmental protection. Since the 1990s special forums on population, resources and the environment have been held to address the population issue by legal, publicity, economic and administrative means through overall planning and coordination, thereby closely integrating economic development, family planning, education and publicity, health improvement, poverty relief, improvement of social security and women's social status, and building of civilized and happy families.

Addressing Population Aging

It's predicted that China's aging population will expand faster during the 12th Five-year Plan period (2011-2015). By 2015, the population aged 60 and above will reach 216 million, accounting for 16.7% of the country's total, with 24 million aged 80 and above accounting for 11.1% of the total aged population; over 50% of urban families will become "empty nests" as their children move away (70% in some large and medium-sized cities), and the number of rural "empty-nesters" will reach 40 million, accounting for 37% of the total rural aged population.

Retirees engaging in health-enriching dance in the park

Population aging will inevitably cause new conflicts and pressures, and pose new challenges for economic and social development. The Chinese government pays great attention to the population aging issue, and has taken multiple measures to safeguard the rights and interests of the elderly, such as accelerating the implementation of the pension insurance system for urban workers, promoting new-type rural pension insurance pilot projects to provide social pension insurance for the agrarian population. To effectively protect the legitimate rights and interests of the elderly and promote undertakings for the aged, the government is formulating the laws on pension insurance, medical insurance, social relief, maintenance of parents, social services, housing and welfare for the elderly, and other special laws and regulations concerning senior citizens.

China energetically advocates the development of market-based multi-layer old-age industries and services under government guidance. All social sectors are encouraged to participate in establishing an operating mechanism which is under government macro-control, launched by non-government efforts, and independently managed by enterprises and institutions in accordance with market requirements.

Ethnic Groups

China is a unitary multi-ethnic nation made up of 56 ethnic groups. Because the Han account for 91.6% of the country's total population, the other 55 are customarily referred to as "ethnic minorities." The Han people live throughout China. The Tibetans mainly live in Tibet Autonomous Region, and Qinghai, Sichuan and Yunnan provinces, the Manchus in northeast China, the Mongolians in Inner Mongolia Autonomous Region, the Uyghurs in Xinjiang Uyghur Autonomous Region, the Hui people in Ningxia Hui Autonomous Region, and the Zhuang people in Guangxi Zhuang Autonomous Region.

A Tibetan girl

A Mongolian
herdsman

A Manchu girl

A Uyghur elder

A Hui child

Ethnic group	Ethnic group
Han	Gelao
Mongol	Xibe
Hui	Achang
Tibetan	Primi
Uyghur	Tajik
Miao	Nu
Yi	Uzbek
Zhuang	Russian
Bouyei	Ewenki
Korean	Deang
Manchu	Boan
Dong	Yugur
Yao	Naxi
Bai	Jingpo
Tujia	Va
Hani	She
Kazak	Gaoshan
Dai	Lahu
Li	Sui
Gin	Tu
Tatar	Daur
Derung	Mulam
Oroqen	Qiang
Hezhen	Blang
Monba	Salar
Lhoba	Maonan
Jino	Lisu
Kirgiz	Dongxiang

Urumqi

Lhasa

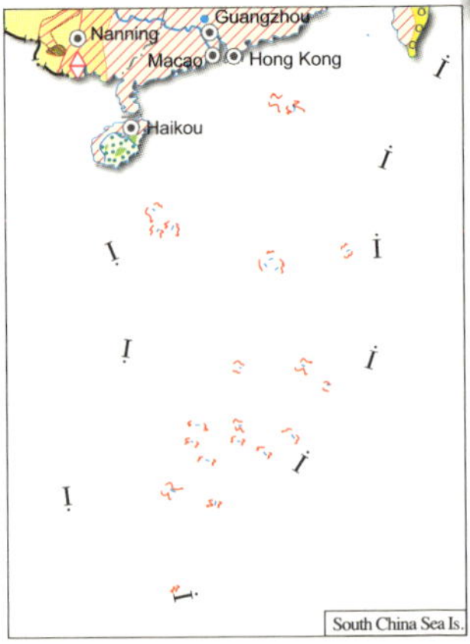

Nanning
Guangzhou
Macao
Hong Kong
Haikou

South China Sea Is.

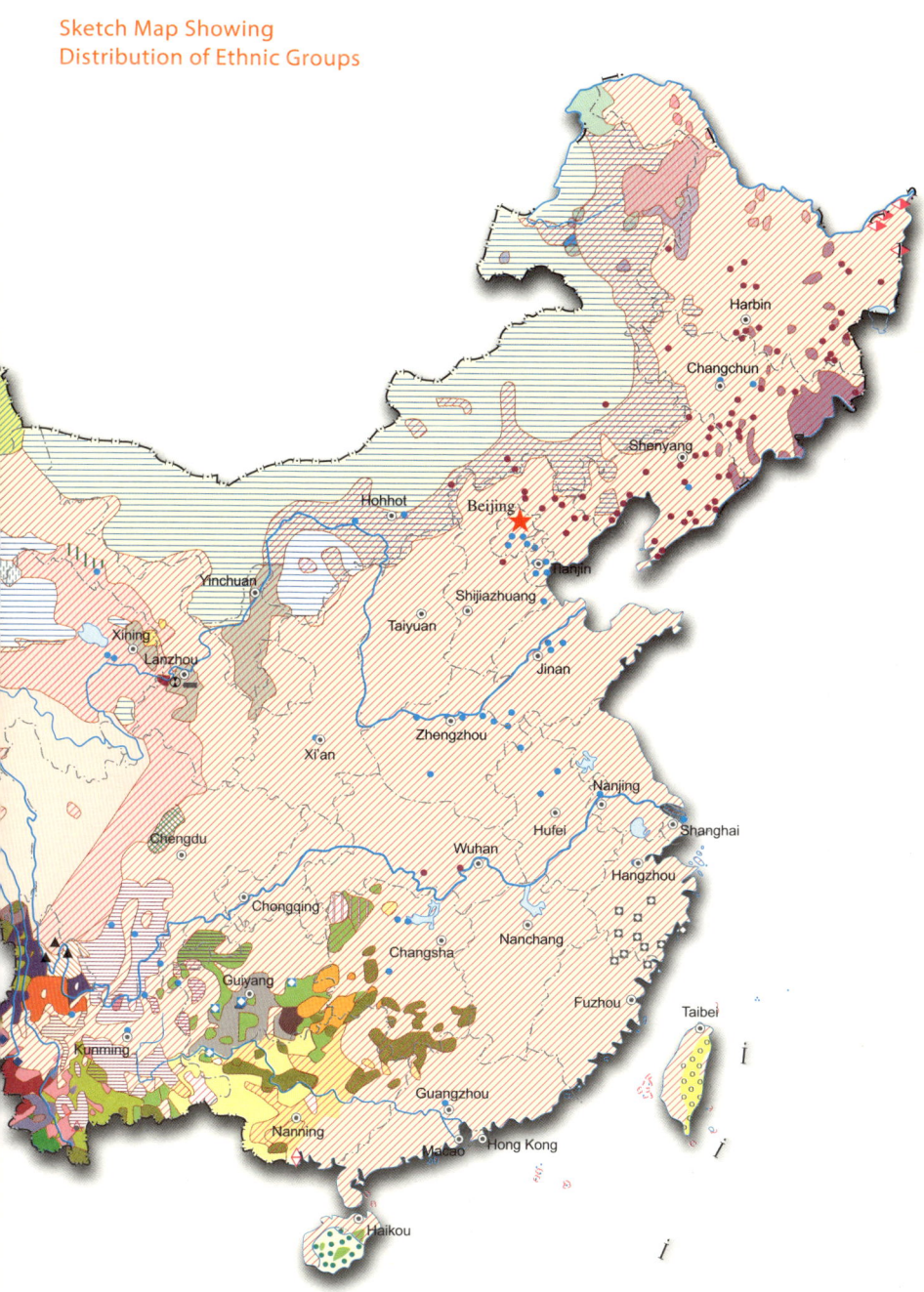

Sketch Map Showing Distribution of Ethnic Groups

Harbin

Changchun

Shenyang

Hohhot

Beijing

Yinchuan

Tianjin

Shijiazhuang

Taiyuan

Xining

Jinan

Lanzhou

Zhengzhou

Xi'an

Nanjing

Hufei

Shanghai

Chengdu

Wuhan

Hangzhou

Chongqing

Changsha

Nanchang

Guiyang

Fuzhou

Taibei

Kunming

Guangzhou

Nanning

Macao

Hong Kong

Haikou

A wedding ceremony of the Miao people

Spoken and Written Languages

Hanyu (spoken Chinese) is the most commonly used language in China, and *Hanzi* (Chinese written characters) is the most commonly used written language. All of China's 55 minority peoples have their own languages, except for the Hui and the Manchu, who only use Chinese; 22 have their own scripts, with 28 scripts in total. Nowadays, schools catering mainly to minority students all use textbooks compiled in their languages, while also teaching *Hanyu* and *Hanzi*.

Written Chinese characters originated from a pictographic system invented by the Chinese people 4,000 years ago, making it the world's oldest form of writing still in use.

Chinese characters include simplified Chinese characters, used on the Chinese mainland and among Chinese communities in Southeast Asia, and traditional Chinese characters, used widely in Hong Kong, Macao, Taiwan Province and among overseas Chinese in North America. In recent years, the use of simplified Chinese characters has grown, as more and more people in other countries are choosing Chinese to study as a second language.

Zhonghua Zihai (*Grand Dictionary of Chinese Characters*), published in 1994, contains more than 85,000 Chinese written characters. The official *Xiandai Hanyu Changyong Zibiao* (*List of Frequently Used Characters in Modern Chinese*), promulgated in 1988, contains 2,500 most frequently used characters and 1,000 in less-common use.

The Only Living Pictographs — Dongba Writing

Dongba writing is the ancient pictographic script of the shamans (Dongba) of China's Naxi ethnic minority, with a history of over 1,000 years. Originally carved on wood and stone, later it came to be written on paper. There are about 1,400 characters in the script, which are still in use. It is the only living pictograph language in the world, and is known as a "living fossil."

Traditional Festivals

China's major traditional festivals are: Spring Festival, Lantern Festival, Qingming Festival, Dragon-boat Festival, and Mid-autumn Festival. The ethnic minorities retain their own traditional festivals, including Ramadan of the Hui people, Kurban of the Uyghur people, Water Sprinkling Festival of the Dai people, Nadam Fair of the Mongolian people, Torch Festival of the Yi People, Danu (Never Forget

Water Sprinkling Festival of the Dai people

the Past) Festival of the Yao people, Third Month Fair of the Bai people, Antiphonal Singing Day of the Zhuang people, New Year and Ongkor (Expecting a Good Harvest) Festival of the Tibetan people, and Jumping Flower Festival of the Miao people.

Spring Festival

In the olden days, when the lunar calendar was in use, the first day of the first lunar month was the beginning of the new year. After the Revolution of 1911 China adopted the Gregorian calendar. To distinguish the lunar New Year's Day from that of the Gregorian calendar, the former came to be called "Spring Festival," which generally falls between the last 10 days of January and mid-February. The Eve of the Spring Festival is an important time for family reunions, when many people stay up all night, "seeing the old year out." During the Spring Festival various traditional activities are enjoyed, including lion dances, dragon lantern dances, land-boat rowing and stilt walking.

Lantern Festival

The Lantern Festival falls on the 15th day of the first lunar month, the first full-moon night after the Spring Festival. Traditionally, people eat *yuanxiao* and admire lanterns on the evening of this day. *Yuanxiao*, round balls of glutinous rice flour with sweet fillings, symbolize reunion. The tradition of admiring lanterns emerged in the first century AD, and is still popular across the country.

Spring Festival shopping

Pure Brightness Festival

The Qingming (Pure Brightness) Festival falls around April 5 every year. Traditionally, this is an occasion for people to make ceremonial offerings to their ancestors. It is also a time to pay respects to revolutionary martyrs. At this time of the year, the weather begins to turn warm and vegetation is bursting into new life. People like to go on outings, fly kites and enjoy the beauty of spring. That is why the festival is also called "Spring Outing Day."

Dragon-boat Festival

The Dragon-boat Festival falls on the fifth day of the fifth lunar month, when the weather is turning warm and insects awake from hibernation. This fes-

Making *zongzi* on the occasion of the Dragon Boat Festival

tival is said to honor the patriotic poet Qu Yuan (c. 340-278 BC) of the State of Chu during the Warring States Period. Failing to realize his political ideals and hold back the decline of his state, Qu Yuan drowned himself in despair in the Miluo River on the fifth day of the fifth lunar month. Every year thereafter, on this day people will go boating on rivers and throw bamboo tubes filled with rice into the water. Today, the memory of Qu Yuan lives on, as *zongzi* (glutinous rice wrapped pyramid-fashion in bamboo or reed leaves) are eaten and dragon-boat races are held.

Mid-autumn Festival

The Mid-autumn Festival falls on the 15th day of the eighth lunar month, in the middle of autumn. In ancient times, people offered pastries or "moon-cakes" as blessings to the Moon Goddess on this day. After the ceremony, the family would sit together to share the "moon-cakes." The festival came to symbolize family reunions, as did the "moon-cakes," and the custom has been passed down to this day.

Religion

China is a country of great religious diversity, with over 100 million followers of various faiths, including Buddhism, Islam, and Christianity (Catholic and Protestant churches), along with China's indigenous Taoism, Shamanism and the Dongba religion of the Naxi people. The number of religious followers keeps increasing stably, and there are about 130,000 places for religious activities across the country.

China pursues a free religious-belief policy. In China, regular religious activities — such as worshiping Buddha, chanting sutras, praying, expounding on the scriptures, celebrating the Mass, baptism, ordination of monks and nuns, and observance of religious festivals — are all managed by religious personnel and adherents themselves, and protected by the law. The holy books of each religion are published and distributed by religious associations. Each religion has its own

Grand Buddhist service in Lhasa

Daoists at Mount Laoshan, Qingdao, Shandong Province

Dongguan Mosque in Xining, Qinghai Province

Catholic church in Nanjing, built by the 16th century Italian missionary Matteo Ricci

A ceremony at the Enguang Protestant Church in Chengdu, Sichuan Province

national periodical, which is also circulated abroad.

National religious associations: Chinese Buddhist Association, Chinese Taoist Association, Chinese Islamic Association, Chinese Patriotic Catholic Association, Chinese Catholic Bishops College, Three-self Patriotic Movement Committee of the Protestant Churches of China and China Christian Council. All these associations elect their leaders and institutions in accordance with their respective charters.

Five Major Religions

Buddhism was introduced to China from India around the first century AD, and became the most influential religion in China after the fourth century. Tibetan Buddhism, a branch of Chinese Buddhism, is primarily practiced in the Tibet and Inner Mongolia autonomous regions.

Taoism is based on the philosophy of Lao Zi, of the Spring and Autumn Period (770-476 BC) and his work *Dao De Jing* (*Classic of the Way and Virtue*).

Islam first reached China around the mid-seventh century, and reached its zenith of prosperity in the Yuan Dynasty (1279-1368). Islam is followed mainly by the Hui, Uyghur and a few other ethnic minorities.

Catholicism was introduced into China in the 17th century, and Protestantism in the early 19th century.

The Great Hall of the People, Beijing

Political System and State Structure

China's political system basically consists of, under the unified leadership of the CPC, the people's congress system, the multiparty cooperation and political consultation system, and the regional ethnic autonomy system. The state organs of the PRC are the NPC, President of the PRC, State Council, Central Military Commission, local people's congresses and local people's governments at various levels, organs of self-government of ethnic autonomous areas, people's courts and people's procuratorates.

The Constitution

Since the founding of the People's Republic of China (PRC) in 1949, four Constitutions have been formulated successively, in 1954, 1975, 1978 and 1982. The present Constitution contains 138 articles. Amendments to the Constitution have been made four times, the last time being in 2004. The Constitution stipulates that all citizens are equal before the law and that the state respects and safeguards human rights. It guarantees the basic rights and interests of citizens, including the right to vote and stand for election; freedom of speech, of the press, of assembly, of association, of procession and of demonstration; freedom of religious belief; the inviolability of the freedom of the person, personal dignity, residence and legitimate private property; freedom and privacy of correspondence; the right to criticize and make suggestions regarding any state organ or functionary, and exercise su-

Four Amendments to the Current Constitution

The 1988 amendment to the Constitution stipulates that the state permits the private sector of the economy to exist and develop within the limits prescribed by law, and the right to the use of land may be transferred in accordance with the law. The 1993 amendment stipulates that the state practices a socialist market economy, and the system of multiparty cooperation and political consultation under the leadership of the CPC will exist and develop for a long time. The 1999 amendment stipulates that the state governs the country by law, and upholds the basic economic system in which public ownership is dominant and diverse forms of ownership develop side by side. The 2004 amendment stipulates that the lawful private property of citizens may not be encroached upon; the state protects by law the right of citizens to own and to inherit private property; the state respects and protects human rights.

Legal System

The overall legislative objective set forth at the 15th CPC National Congress in 1997 pointed out that a socialist system of laws with Chinese characteristics would be established by 2010. By that year China had formulated 239 general laws, over 690 administrative laws and regulations, and 8,600-plus local regulations.

China's legal system, dominated by the Constitution and with Constitution-related laws, civil laws, commercial laws, administrative laws, economic laws, social laws, criminal laws and procedural laws as the main branches, consists of the multi-layered laws, administrative laws and regulations and local regulations governing the economic, political, cultural and social aspects.

pervision; the right to work and rest, and the right to material assistance from the state and society when old, ill or disabled; and the right to receive education, and freedom to engage in scientific research, literary and artistic creation, and other cultural pursuits.

Political System

The basic structure of China's political system consists of, under the unified leadership of the Communist Party of China (CPC), the people's congress system, the multiparty cooperation and political consultation system, and the ethnic regional autonomy system.

People's Congress System

In China, the organs through which the people exercise state power are the National People's Congress (NPC) and local people's congresses. Therefore, the people's congress system is China's fundamental political system. Its basic feature is adherence to the principle of democratic centralism, i.e., the people enjoy extensive democracy and rights, while state power is exercised in a centralized and unified way. On the premise that the people's congresses exercise state power in a unified way, the state's administrative power, judicial authority, procuratorial authority and leadership over the armed forces are clearly divided, so as to ensure that the organs of state power and administrative, judicial and procuratorial and other state organs work in a coordinated way.

Deputies to the people's congresses at all levels are elected. They include people from all ethnic groups, all walks of life, all regions and all social strata. When the congresses meet they can air their views fully; they can also raise inquiries to governments at the corresponding level and their affiliated departments, and the parties concerned are duty-bound to reply to the inquiries. Electors or constituencies have the right to recall their elected deputies in accordance with the procedures prescribed by law.

Multiparty Cooperation and Political Consultation System

China is a country with multiple political parties. Before the state adopts important measures or makes decisions on major issues with a bearing on the national economy and the people's well-being, the CPC, as the party in power, consults with representatives of all political parties, as well as people without party affiliation. This system of multiparty cooperation and political consultation led by the CPC is the basic political system of China.

Multiparty cooperation and political consultation take two principal forms: (1) Chinese People's Political Consultative Conference (CPPCC); and (2) consultative meetings and forums with the participation of people from non-Communist parties and people without party affiliation, at the invitation of the CPC.

The CPPCC National Committee consists of representatives of the CPC, non-Communist parties, people without party affiliation, people's organizations, ethnic minorities and other social strata, and specially invited individuals. The CPPCC National Committee is elected for a term of five years. In addition to attending a plenary session once a year, its members are invited to audit the annual NPC session and fully air their views as non-voting delegates, so as to exercise the functions of political consultation, democratic supervision and participation in the deliberation and administration of state affairs. Once a year, leaders of the CPC Central Committee invite leaders of the non-Communist parties and representatives of people without party affiliation to consultative meetings, and forums are held every other month. The former focuses on major state policies, the latter on exchange of information, receiving policy proposals and discussing special issues.

Regional Ethnic Autonomy System

China practices a regional ethnic autonomy system. Where minorities live in compact communities, organs of self-government are established under the unified leadership of the state. As masters in their own areas, minority people exercise auton-

Minority delegates attending the NPC and the CPPCC sessions

omous power, and administer their own internal affairs. The Central Government actively aids the ethnic autonomous areas with funds and materials, so as to promote the development of local economies and cultures. The Law on Regional Ethnic Autonomy, adopted in 1984 at the Second Session of the Sixth NPC, is the basic law guaranteeing the implementation of the regional ethnic autonomy system.

In addition to the five autonomous regions (Inner Mongolia, Xinjiang Uyghur, Guangxi Zhuang, Ningxia Hui and Tibet), China has 30 autonomous prefectures, 120 autonomous counties (banners) and over 1,100 ethnic townships. The organs of self-government in ethnic autonomous areas are the people's congresses and people's governments of autonomous regions, autonomous prefectures, and autonomous counties (banners). The chairperson or vice-chairs of the standing committee of the people's congress and the head of an autonomous region, autonomous prefecture or autonomous county (banner) should be citizens of the community exercising regional autonomy in the area concerned.

Organs of self-government in ethnic autonomous areas enjoy extensive self-government powers beyond those held by other state organs at the same level. These include: enacting regulations on the exercise of autonomy and separate regulations corresponding to the political, economic and cultural characteristics of the ethnic group(s) in the areas concerned; having the freedom to manage and use all revenues accruing to the ethnic autonomous areas; independently arranging and managing local economic development, education, science, culture, public health and physical culture, protecting their cultural heritage, and developing their cultures.

National People's Congress

The NPC, the highest organ of state power, consists of deputies elected by all provinces, autonomous regions, municipalities directly under the Central Government, special administrative regions, and the armed forces. It exercises legislative power and makes decisions on major issues regarding national political life. Its main functions and powers are enacting and amending laws; examining and approving national economic and social development plans, state budgets and reports on their implementation; making decisions on matters of war and peace; electing and choosing the leadership of the highest organs of state, i.e. electing the Chairman of the Standing Committee of the NPC, the President of the PRC, the Premier of the State Council, and the Chairman of the Central Military Commission, with the power to recall any of the above mentioned.

The NPC is elected for a term of five years, and is now in its 11th term. The current Chairman of the NPC Standing Committee is **Wu Bangguo**.

Presidency

Working together with the NPC Standing Committee, the President of the PRC exercises his or her functions and powers as the head of state. The President, pursuant to decisions of the NPC or its Standing Committee, promulgates laws, appoints and removes members of the State Council, and issues orders; on behalf of the PRC, conducts state activities, receives foreign diplomatic representatives, dispatches and recalls plenipotentiary representatives abroad, and ratifies or abrogates treaties and important agreements reached with foreign states. The current President is **Hu Jintao**.

State Council

The State Council is the Central People's Government. It is the executive body of the highest organ of state power (the NPC), and the highest state administrative body. The State Council is responsible to the NPC and its Standing Committee, and reports to them on its work. The State Council has the power to formulate administrative measures, enact administrative regulations, and promulgate decisions and orders within its functions and powers. The State Council is composed of the Premier, Vice Premiers, State Councilors, Secretary-general, Ministers in charge of ministries, Ministers in charge of commissions, Governor of the People's Bank of China, and Auditor-general of the National Audit Office. The current Premier is **Wen Jiabao**.

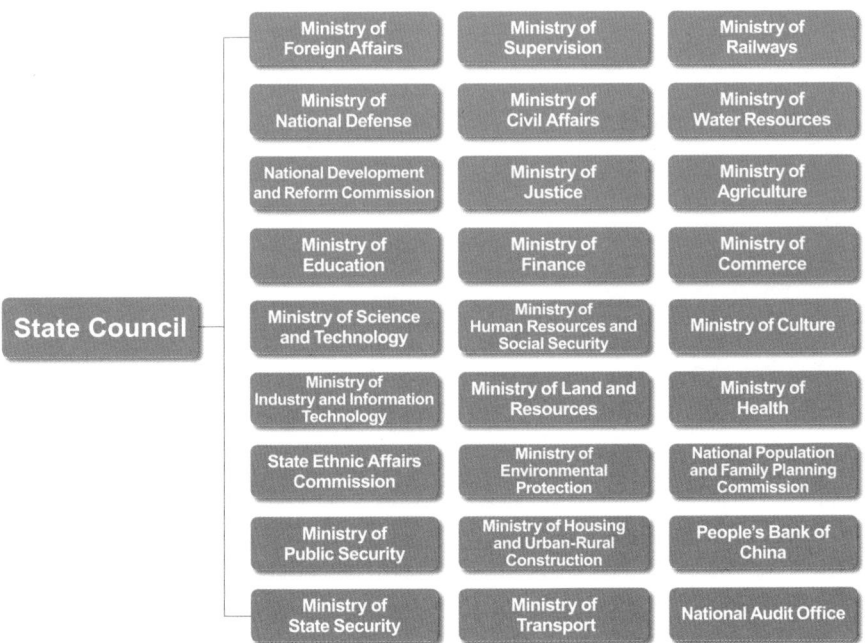

Central Military Commission

The Central Military Commission is the nation's leading organ and commander of the armed forces. China's armed forces consist of the Chinese People's Liberation Army (PLA), the Chinese People's Armed Police Force, and the Militia. The PLA is the standing army of the state. The main tasks of the Armed Police Force include performing guard duties and maintaining public order, as empowered by the state. The Militia is an armed force of the masses and, when not on duty, remains engaged in normal productive activities. The Central Military Commission is composed of the Chair, Vice Chairs and other members. The current Chairman is **Hu Jintao**.

China pursues a national defense policy which is defensive in nature. In accordance with the Constitution and other relevant laws, the armed forces undertake the sacred duty of resisting foreign aggression, defending the motherland, and safeguarding overall social stability and the peaceful labor of its people. To build a fortified national defense and strong armed forces compatible with national security and development interests is a strategic task of China's modernization, and a common cause of the people of all ethnic groups.

The goals and tasks of China's national defense in the new era: safeguarding national sovereignty and security, and the interests of national development; maintaining social harmony and stability; accelerating the modernization of national defense and the armed forces; and maintaining world peace and stability.

China's National Defense in 2010 (White Paper)

On March 31, 2010, the Chinese government published *China's National Defense in 2010*. It is the seventh White Paper on national defense published since 1998. These White Papers elaborate China's national defense policy, construction of national defense and the armed forces, so as to give the international community a better introduction to China and the Chinese armed forces, and to promote mutual trust and cooperation between China and the rest of the world.

China's National Defense in 2010 emphasizes four points: First, China unswervingly takes the road of peaceful development, and pursues a national defense policy which is defensive in nature; second, China promotes the balanced development of national defense and economic construction, so as to build a well-off country with powerful armed forces in the course of building a moderately prosperous society in all respects; third, China actively promotes military exchanges and cooperation, and military confidence-building with other countries; and fourth, China performs its international responsibilities and obligations to safeguard world peace and stability.

Honor guards of the PLA

Local People's Congresses and Local People's Governments

Reflecting existing national administrative divisions, there are people's congresses and people's governments at all levels – in provinces, autonomous regions and municipalities directly under the Central Government; in counties and cities; in townships and towns. The people's congresses at and above the county level have standing committees.

The local people's congresses are the local organs of state power. They have the power to decide on important affairs in their respective administrative areas. The people's congresses of provinces, autonomous regions and municipalities directly under the Central Government have the power to formulate local regulations. Local people's governments are the local administrative organs. Working under the unified leadership of the State Council, they are responsible to and report on their work to the people's congresses and their standing committees at the corresponding level and to the organs of state administration at the next higher level. They have overall responsibility for the administrative work within their respective administrative areas.

People's Courts

The people's courts are the judicial organs of the state. The Supreme People's Court is established at the state level; higher people's courts are established in provinces, autonomous regions and municipalities directly under the Central Government; and intermediate and primary-level people's courts at lower levels. The Supreme People's Court, the state's highest judicial organ, reports to the NPC and its Standing Committee, and supervises the judicial work of the local people's courts. The current President of the Supreme People's Court is **Wang Shengjun**.

People's Procuratorates

The people's procuratorates are state organs of legal supervision. Their organization corresponds to that of the people's courts. The people's procuratorates have the right to exercise procuratorial authority. They exercise this authority over cases endangering state and public security, damaging economic order and infringing on citizens' personal and democratic rights, as well as over other important criminal cases; examine cases scheduled for investigation by public security agencies, and decide on whether suspects should be arrested or not, and whether cases should be prosecuted or exempt from prosecution; institute and support public prosecution in criminal cases; and oversee the activities of public security agencies, people's courts, prisons, houses of detention, and reform-through-labor institutions. The current Procurator-general of the Supreme People's Procuratorate is **Cao Jianming**.

The NPC, the CPPCC and the State Council

The NPC exercises power through election, ballot and voting, fully consulting the CPPCC before elections and voting. These are the two most important manifestations of China's socialist democracy. The relationship between the NPC, the CPPCC and the State Council is that the CPPCC is consulted before policymaking, after which the NPC votes on policymaking, and the State Council is responsible for policy implementation. They fulfill their separate duties with full cooperation and mutual reliance, while complementing each other under the unified leadership of the CPC. This political system with Chinese characteristics is suited to China's actual conditions.

Chinese People's Political Consultative Conference

The CPPCC is an organization of the Chinese people's patriotic united front as well as an important institution of multiparty cooperation and political consultation under the leadership of the CPC. It is an important channel for promoting socialist democracy in China's political life.

The main functions of the CPPCC are: political consultation, democratic supervision, and participation in the deliberation and administration of state affairs.

The CPPCC has its National Committee and local committees.

CPPCC National Committee

The CPPCC National Committee consists of members of the CPC and non-Communist parties, people without party affiliation, representatives of people's organizations, ethnic minorities and all walks of life, representatives of the Hong Kong and Macao special administrative regions, Taiwan Province and returned overseas Chinese, and specially invited individuals.

The CPPCC National Committee is elected for a term of five years, and is now in its 11th term. The Chairman of the 11th CPPCC National Committee is **Jia Qinglin**.

CPPCC Local Committees

CPPCC committees have been set up in all provinces, autonomous regions, municipalities directly under the Central Government; autonomous prefectures and cities divided into districts; counties, autonomous counties, cities not divided into districts and districts under the jurisdiction of cities.

Political Parties and Other Organizations

Communist Party of China

Founded in July 1921, the CPC had more than 80.26 million members by the end of 2010.

From 1921 to 1949 the CPC led the Chinese people in their arduous struggle that finally brought about the expulsion of the Japanese aggressors and the establishment of the People's Republic of China (PRC). Then it led the Chinese people in carrying out systematic large-scale socialist construction. The CPC's lack of experience led to some errors in leading the process of constructing socialism, followed by the serious mistake of launching the "cultural revolution" (1966-1976).

The "cultural revolution" ended in October 1976, at which turning point China entered a new historic era of development. Following the Third Plenary Session of the 11th CPC Central Committee at the end of 1978, the country embarked on the biggest change in the history of New China. Since 1979 China's economic and social development has been crowned with remarkable success.

The highest leading organ of the CPC is the National Congress, which is held once every five years. When the National Congress is not in session, the Central Committee implements its decisions and leads all the work of the Party. From October 15 to 21, 2007 the CPC held its 17th National Congress, reviewing and summarizing the historical course and valuable experience of

July 23, 1921, the 1st National Congress of the CPC was held at No. 106 Wangzhi Road in the French Concession of Shanghai (now No. 76 Xingye Road), marking the founding of the CPC

China's reform and opening up, and putting forward major policies and specific goals for the new period. The Congress also amended the Party Constitution and elected the new Central Committee members. The current General Secretary of the CPC Central Committee is **Hu Jintao**.

The core of the CPC's governing concept is putting people first and serving the people wholeheartedly. The main contents include: to build the Party for the public interest and exercise governance for the people; exercise government power in a scientific, democratic and law-based manner, as a ruling party that is realistic, pragmatic and hardworking, yet effective, open, clean and committed to reform and innovation; and lead all the Chinese people to strive for the country's prosperity, national rejuvenation, social harmony and the well-being of all.

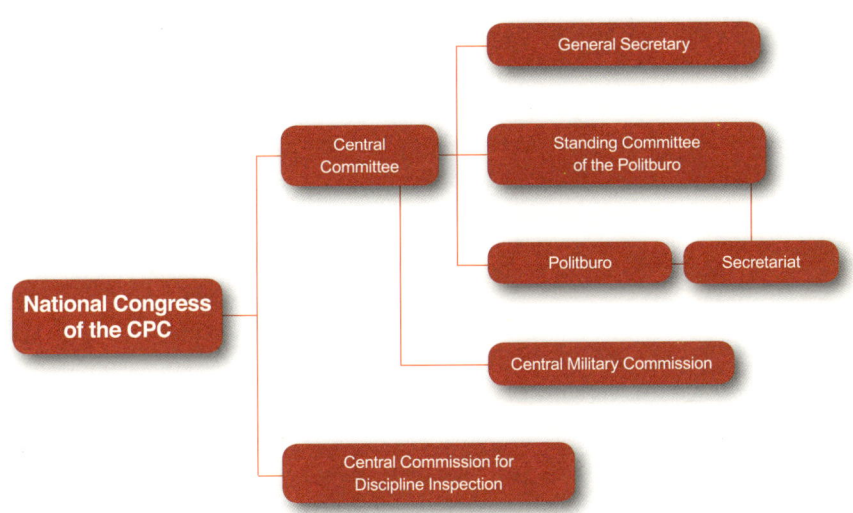

Non-Communist Parties

Besides the CPC, China has eight other political parties. These parties all support the CPC's political leadership, and enjoy political freedom, organizational independence and lawful equality within the scope of the Constitution. The basic principle of the cooperation between the CPC and the other parties is long-term coexistence, mutual supervision, treating each other with sincerity and sharing each other's weal and woe.

Many of the members of these parties hold posts on the standing committees of the people's congresses, CPPCC committees, government organs, and economic, cultural, educational, scientific and technological departments. For instance, the chairpersons of the eight parties' central committees are currently vice-chairs of the NPC Standing Committee or the CPPCC National Committee. With a combined membership exceeding 700,000, they have set up branches and primary-level organizations in all provinces, autonomous regions and municipalities directly under the Central Government, and in large and medium-sized cities.

The Eight Non-communist Parties:

Revolutionary Committee of the Chinese Kuomintang

Established in January 1948

Former members of the KMT and people having historical connections with the KMT

Chairperson: **Zhou Tienong**

China Democratic League

Established in October 1941

Higher and mid-level intellectuals

Chairperson: **Jiang Shusheng**

China Democratic National Construction Association

Established in December 1945

Specialists, scholars and other people in the economic field

Chairperson: **Chen Changzhi**

China Association for Promoting Democracy

Established in December 1945

Intellectuals working in educational, cultural, scientific, publishing and other fields

Chairperson: **Yan Junqi**

Chinese Peasants and Workers Democratic Party

Established in August 1930

Higher and mid-level intellectuals in the fields of medicine, culture, education, and science and technology

Chairperson: **Sang Guowei**

China Zhi Gong Dang

Established in October 1925

Returned overseas Chinese, relatives of overseas Chinese, representative individuals, specialists, and scholars with overseas connections

Chairperson: **Wan Gang**

Jiusan Society

Established in December 1944

Higher and mid-level intellectuals working in fields of science and technology, culture, education and public health

Chairperson: **Han Qide**

Taiwan Democratic Self-government League

Established in November 1947

People born or with family roots in Taiwan Province currently residing on the mainland

Chairperson: **Lin Wenyi**

Mass Organizations and NGOs

Chinese mass organizations carry out their activities independently and in accordance with the Constitution and the law. Their branches cover urban and rural areas. They participate in national and local political life, and play an important role in coordinating social and public affairs, and safeguarding the legitimate rights and interests of the people.

Chinese NGOs are mainly engaged in technology, education, culture, health, sports, environmental protection, legal services, and intermediary services. Environmental NGOs have become an important force in popularizing environmental education and promoting public participation. Their joining the government to promote environmental protection has been a major characteristic and trend in the field.

Major Mass Organizations:

All-China Federation of Trade Unions

Established in May 1925

Workers

Chairman: **Wang Zhaoguo**

All-China Youth Federation

Established in May 1949

Youth from all walks of life

First Secretary: **Wang Xiao**

All-China Women's Federation

Established in April 1949

Women from all walks of life

Chairwoman: **Chen Zhili**

All-China Federation of Industry and Commerce

Established in October 1953

People in the non-public economic sectors

Chairman: **Huang Mengfu**

The national flags of the countries participating in the Shanghai 2010 Expo.

Foreign Relations

Since 1949, the People's Republic of China has unswervingly pursued an independent foreign policy of peace. It is committed to developing friendship and cooperation with neighboring countries, developing countries and the major powers on the basis of the Five Principles of Peaceful Coexistence. As a permanent member of the UN Security Council, China plays an increasingly important role on the stage of multilateral diplomacy in an all-round, multilevel and wide-ranging manner. Acting as a responsible country, it makes great efforts to improve multilateral cooperation and promote the settlement of disputes.

Foreign Policy

China pursues an independent foreign policy of peace, follows the path of peaceful development, adheres to a mutually-beneficial open strategy, and endeavors to build a harmonious world of lasting peace and common prosperity. It is committed to developing friendship and cooperation with all other countries on the basis of the Five Principles of Peaceful Coexistence. It will continue to safeguard its sovereignty, security and territorial integrity, to finally realize the great cause of peaceful reunification of the whole country. It will continue developing economic diplomacy, cultural diplomacy and public diplomacy, vigorously expanding economic cooperation with other countries, increasing dialogues and communications between civilizations and gaining more understanding from the international community. It insists on the principle of "people first" and "people-oriented diplomacy," safeguarding the legitimate rights and interests of Chinese citizens and legal persons in other countries.

Harmonious World

At the Asian-African Summit held in Jakarta in April 2005 President Hu Jintao for the first time declared the idea of "jointly constructing a harmonious world." He elaborated systematically on this new idea of "building a harmonious world of lasting peace and common prosperity" later, at the convention of the 60th anniversary of the United Nations on September 15, 2005.

In the report to the 17th National Congress of the CPC in 2007, he pointed out, "We maintain that the people of all countries should join hands and strive to build a harmonious world of lasting peace and common prosperity. To this end, all countries should uphold the purposes and principles of the United Nations Charter, observe international law and universally recognized norms of international relations, and promote democracy, harmony, collaboration and win-win solutions in international relations. Politically, all countries should respect each other and conduct consultations on an equal footing in a common endeavor to promote democracy in international relations. Economically, they should cooperate with each other, draw on each other's strengths and work together to advance economic globalization in the direction of balanced development, shared benefits and win-win progress. Culturally, they should learn from each other in the spirit of seeking common ground while shelving differences, respect the diversity of the world, and make joint efforts to advance human civilization. In the area of security, they should trust each other, strengthen cooperation, settle international disputes by peaceful means rather than by war, and work together to safeguard peace and stability in the world. On environmental issues, they should assist and cooperate with each other in conservation efforts to take good care of the Earth, the only home of human beings."

Friendship with Neighboring Countries

China follows a policy of friendship and partnership with neighboring countries. It improves friendly and practical cooperation with them, actively carries out regional cooperation, and works with them to jointly create a stable, peaceful regional environment based on equality, mutual trust and mutually beneficial cooperation.

China maintains close high-level contacts with neighboring countries. In 2010 Chinese leaders visited Russia, Kazakhstan, Cambodia, Indonesia, Thailand, the ROK, Japan, Mongolia, Myanmar, India, Pakistan, Iran, Bangladesh, Laos, Singapore and the DPRK. Leaders of Russia, the DPRK, Myanmar and Singapore also visited China.

China develops economic relations featuring mutual benefit with neighboring countries. By far, China is the largest trading partner of Russia, Kazakhstan, Japan, the ROK, India, Vietnam, Mongolia and the ASEAN. China strengthens its cooperation with neighboring countries based on equality and mutual benefit, deepens regional and sub-regional economic cooperation, and actively promotes regional integration. Through joint efforts, Asian countries have overcome the impacts of the international financial crisis, which started in 2008. The Asian economy grew

The China-ASEAN Expo and China-ASEAN Business & Investment Summit opening in Nanning, Guangxi Zhuang Autonomous Region

by 8.2% in 2010, becoming an important engine driving the global economic recovery.

China actively participates in and promotes the process of regional integration. When attending the SCO summits, ASEAN Plus China summit, ASEAN Plus Three (China, Japan and the ROK) summit, East Asian Summit and leaders' meeting of China, Japan and the ROK, Chinese leaders had extensive contacts with leaders of other countries and communicated closely with them, playing an positive role in consolidating neighborly relations, deepening regional cooperation and promoting common progress.

China adheres to a new concept of security based on mutual trust, mutual benefit, equality and cooperation. It endeavors to resolve, through dialogue and negotiation, all land and sea territorial disputes with neighboring countries. Concerning serious issues, China has mediated in negotiations between the parties concerned, in order to achieve peace and stability in Asia.

China and the ASEAN

China initiated dialogue with the ASEAN in 1991, and in 2003 it became the first country outside the region to join the Friendly Cooperation Treaty of Southeast Asia, establishing with the ASEAN a strategic partnership aiming at peace and prosperity. So far, a relatively complete mechanism for dialogue and cooperation has been set up between the two sides, including a summit, 11 ministerial meetings and five executive meetings. The ASEAN-China Free Trade Area was set up in 2010. The ASEAN has become the fourth biggest trading partner of China.

The year 2011 is the 20th anniversary of the establishment of dialogue between China and the ASEAN. The two sides will further deepen their friendship and mutual understanding, actively promote regional cooperation and push forward the common progress of Asia.

Cooperation with Developing Countries

As the world's largest developing country, China takes consolidating and developing mutually beneficial cooperation with other developing countries as a cornerstone of its foreign policy. It endeavors to enhance cooperation with them, deepen traditional friendship, expand practical cooperation, provide them with any aid it can offer, and support the rightful claims and common interests of developing countries.

The Chinese government thinks highly of its friendly relations with India and Pakistan, two of its major neighboring countries. At their invitations, Premier Wen Jiabao made formal visits to India and Pakistan in December 2010, which strengthened Sino-India and Sino-Pakistan strategic partnerships.

On May 13, 2010, the fourth ministerial meeting of the CASCF convening in Tianjin, with many Chinese and foreign reporters attending

China enlists mutually-beneficial cooperation with African countries in economy, politics, culture and other fields. In order to further strengthen friendship and cooperation in the new situation, tackle the challenges presented by economic globalization and promote common development, the Forum for China and Africa Cooperation was founded in 2000, and has become a major platform for multilateral dialogues and an effective mechanism for practical cooperation between China and friendly African countries. Within the framework of the forum, China and Africa have enhanced their mutually beneficial cooperation, taking a series of major measures, like cancelling debts, exempting goods from customs duties, encouraging mutual investments, developing human resources, promoting medical and health care cooperation, implementing tourism cooperation and expanding cultural exchanges.

The China-Arab States Cooperation Forum (CASCF) has been progressing smoothly. The fourth ministerial meeting of the CASCF, held in Tianjin in May 2010, signed a series of important documents for establishing strategic cooperation between China and the Arab states. Under the CASCF framework, the two sides are constantly expanding their friendly and mutually beneficial cooperation in many fields, including politics, economy, trade, energy and culture.

The comprehensive partnership based on equality, mutual benefit and common progress between China and the Latin American countries keeps expanding and deepening. Leaders of the two sides frequently exchange visits, promoting political mutual trust and coordination in world affairs. The trade volume between China and Latin America exceeded US$180 billion-worth in 2010, up 50.2% over 2009, marking the fastest

China-Arab States Cooperation Forum

China has established diplomatic relations with all 22 Arab countries. The friendly cooperation in various fields between China and the Arab states has kept developing. To tap the cooperation potential, the CASCF was founded on January 30, 2004. A dozen cooperative mechanisms in the fields of politics, economy and culture have been set up.

growth of China's trade with a major region. The mutually beneficial cooperation between the two sides in such fields as finance, investment, energy, mining, capital construction, agriculture and high technology is making new progress. Cultural exchanges and cooperation are also fruitful.

Cooperation with Major Countries

China adheres to the policy of promoting strategic dialogue, enhancing mutual trust and deepening cooperation with the world's major powers, and resolving divergences in an appropriate way, based on the Five Principles of Peaceful Coexistence to promote long-term, stable and sound bilateral relations.

Sino-US Relations

China is the world's largest developing country, and the US is the largest developed country. The relationship between China and the US is one of the most important bilateral relationships in the world today. A good relationship serves the common interests of the two countries and the peace, stability and prosperity of the whole world.

In recent years presidents of the two countries have exchanged state visits. They have met on multiple occasions at international conferences and in multilateral activities, and keep contact through telephone calls and letters. By such measures, they exchange views on Sino-US relations and other major international and regional issues of common concern, and have reached consensus on many issues. When President Hu Jintao paid a state visit to the US in January 2011 the two countries issued a joint statement, saying that "China and the United States are committed to work together to build a cooperative partnership based on mutual respect and mutual benefit."

On May 9, 2010, the third round of the China-US Strategic and Economic Dialogue opening in Washington

The two countries have a close economic and trade relationship, as each other's second largest trading partner. Among all major trading partners, China is the one to which the US exports are growing the fastest. China and the US have realized progress in cooperation in fields like economy, finance, energy, non-proliferation, law enforcement, environmental protection and culture, and achieved fruitful results in the course of contacts and coordination in both international and regional issues. Many cooperative mechanisms for dialogue, like the China-US Strategic and Economic Dialogue and the China-US High-level Consultation on People-to-People Exchanges, have been established.

Sino-Russian Relations

In recent years the strategic partnership of coordination between the two countries has matured. China was the first country outside the Commonwealth of Independent States that Russian President Dmitry Medvedev visited after assuming the presidency. Leaders of the two countries meet frequently, exchanging views on bilateral relations and other significant issues of common concern, and reaching consensus on many issues. Both sides have expressed their will to deepen cooperation in the fields of economy, science, technology, energy and culture and continue strengthening their coordination in international and regional affairs.

On April 27, 2010, Russian students performing a Chinese dance *The Qinghai-Tibet Plateau* at the "Chinese Language Year" launched in Amur, Russia

President Hu Jintao met and exchanged views on bilateral relations and other significant issues of common concern with Russian President Medvedev when he attended the second BRIC Summit in April 2010, at which the two sides reached an agreement to promote Sino-Russian strategic partnership of coordination. Russian President Medvedev paid a state visit to China in September that year, and signed with President Hu Jintao Sino-Russian Joint Statement on Comprehensively Deepening the Strategic Partnership of Coordination.

China and Russia are also increasing their cooperation in the cultural field. Through various cultural activities, including the Russian Language Year held in China and the Chinese Language Year held in Russia, the two countries have improved mutual understanding and trust, and consolidated the social foundation for good relations.

China-EU Relations

China established formal diplomatic relations with the European Economic Community in 1975. A multidirectional, multilevel and wide-ranging mutually beneficial cooperation pattern has formed between the two sides through 30-odd years of development.

The leaders of the two sides pay frequent visits to each other, which constantly strengthens their mutual trust in the field of politics. Through various leaders' meetings, the two sides have reached an agreement to deepen the comprehensive strategic partnership to deal with the challenges in the process of globalization, and have signed cooperation documents, in such fields as economy, trade, science, technology and climate change.

Sino-EU cooperation in economy and trade keeps advancing. The China-EU High-level Economic and Trade Dialogue was initiated in April 2008. At present, China is the largest source of the EU's imports and second largest trading partner, while the EU is China's largest trading partner.

China and the EU have gained fruitful results from dialogues and cooperation in the fields of science, technology, education, finance, banking and social security. The two sides have also strengthened their communication and cooperation concerning various global issues, like prevention and control of new-type diseases, energy, food, and climate change.

On February 24, 2011, China-EU Internet of Things Summit in Wuxi, Jiangsu Province

A convenience store in Ōfunato, Japan provided the CISAR team with various supplies. When parting on March 15, 2011, the peoples of the two countries shook hands to express their mutual appreciation.

Sino-Japanese Relations

Japan is a close neighbor of China, and relations with Japan are an important aspect of China's diplomacy. Though there are still some sensitive issues between the two countries, the two sides still keep close contacts and cooperation in economy, trade and culture. Nongovernmental communications are also moving ahead, which improve understanding between the two.

The year 2008 was the 30th anniversary of the signing of the China-Japan Treaty of Peace and Friendship. In May of that year, Chinese President Hu Jintao visited Japan, the first visit in a decade by a Chinese president to Japan. The China-Japan Joint Statement on Comprehensively Promoting Strategic Mutually Beneficial Relations was promulgated, mapping out the future of bilateral relations.

Shanghai's Expo 2010 created a good opportunity for the two countries to conduct communications in various fields such as economy, culture, and science and technology. Some 534,000 Japanese visited the Expo, the second biggest source of overseas visitors.

When Japan suffered a devastating earthquake and tsunami on March 11, 2011 the Chinese government and its people expressed their sympathy and solicitude to the Japanese people. President Hu Jintao went to the Japanese Embassy in Beijing in person to extend his condolences. The Chinese government provided the Japanese government with 30 million yuan-worth humanitarian relief supplies and 20,000 tons of fuel oil. The China International Search and Rescue Team (CISAR) arrived in Japan on March 13 to offer help.

China's International Rescue Work

In participating in international affairs and enlisting international cooperation, China takes humanitarian disaster relief as a public diplomacy measure. The CISAR, comprising mainly soldiers, earthquake experts and medical personnel, was founded in 2001. It primarily serves international humanitarian missions, especially search and rescue for earthquake and other disaster victims. By the end of March 2011 it had undertaken eight international missions.

World Expo Diplomacy

The 41st World Expo was held in Shanghai from May 1 to October 31, 2010. This grand international gathering was also a diplomatic fair that attracted international attention. Representatives of 246 countries and international organizations, over 100 state or government leaders and other important guests attended various activities of the Expo. The participating countries held "national pavilion days," summit forums and information briefings.

Through World Expo diplomacy, China displayed its image as a pursuer of peaceful development, promoted mutual understanding and cooperation among various countries, and realized mutually beneficial results with all countries benefiting from the development of human civilization.

The China Pavilion at the 2010 Expo in Shanghai

Actively Participating in Multilateral Affairs

Since the People's Republic of China resumed its rightful seat in the UN in 1971, it has become increasingly active in multilateral diplomacy. China vigorously participates in multilateral affairs, undertakes its relevant international obligations, plays a constructive role, puts forward proper solutions to major, hot and global issues, and advocates the establishment of a just and rational international order. As a permanent member of the UN Security Council, China takes a more and more important position in mediating thorny international and regional issues, solving global problems and safeguarding world peace. It has formed a responsible image as a big country.

China and the UN

As a permanent member of the UN Security Council, China is committed to safeguarding the primary purposes and principles of the UN Charter, and advocating peaceful solutions to international disputes through dialogue and negotiation. China implements international cooperation in a wide-range of fields, supports UN and Security Council reforms, promotes the campaign to meet the UN Mil-

On December 20, 2010, China's seventh peacekeeping medical team conducting a drill in the Sudan

lennium Development Goals, positively drives the reform of the international financial system, and makes joint efforts with other countries to deal with global challenges like climate change, energy safety and proliferation of weapons of mass destruction.

In September 2010 Premier Wen Jiabao attended a series of UN conferences on invitation, including the UN High-level Meeting on the Millennium Development Goals, the general debate of the 65th Session of the UN General Assembly, and a meeting of leaders from the UN Security Council member states. Wen's trip increased the international community's understanding of China, encouraged the international community to achieve the Millennium Development Goals, and displayed China's image as a nation pursuing peace and stability. China also endeavored to push forward the Cancun Climate Conference in 2010. Its sincerity and efforts in carbon emission reduction were applauded by most other countries.

China consistently supports and actively participates in UN peacekeeping missions. The number of peacekeeping personnel from China is one of the biggest among all Security Council permanent members. From 1989 when China joined a UN peacekeeping mission for the first time, to December 2010 China participated in 19 UN peacekeeping missions, assigning 17,390 officers and soldiers to such missions, with nine peacekeepers sacrificed.

China and the APEC

Established in 1989, the Asia-Pacific Economic Cooperation (APEC) is the highest and most influential economic cooperative mechanism in the Asia-Pacific region. China thinks highly of the role played by the APEC. It always supports and takes an active part in cooperation with it at various levels and in various fields, making significant contributions to APEC's continuous progress.

At the 18th APEC Economic Leaders' Informal Meeting, held in Yokohama, Japan, from November 13 to 14, 2010, President Hu Jintao stated China's views and proposals on many important issues, such as developing an APEC community in which growth is more balanced, inclusive, sustainable, innovative and secure, trade and investment are freer and easier, economic and technological cooperation is further strengthened, and regional economic integration is speeded up. He gave an all-round introduction to China's efforts for achieving scientific and harmonious development, transforming the pattern of economic growth, unswervingly adhering to the path of peaceful development and pursuing a mutually beneficial open strategy. He also advocated the idea of building a harmonious Asia-Pacific region.

On November 13, 2010, the 18th APEC Economic Leaders' Informal
Meeting opening in Yokohama, Japan

The President also participated in the APEC CEO Summit and a dialogue between the leaders of the APEC forum and representatives of the APEC Business Advisory Council. In his speeches, he reviewed the contributions made by developing countries, especially emerging economies, to world economic growth, called for further progress in global economic governance reform, and enlarging developing economies' right to speak and representativeness. He also elaborated on China's open, responsible and sustainable development pattern and the opportunities it brings for business circles in the Asia-Pacific region.

China and the SCO

The Shanghai Five mechanism was formally created on April 26, 1996 when the heads of state of China, Russia, Kazakhstan, Kyrgyzstan and Tajikistan met in Shanghai for the first time. The Shanghai Cooperation Organization (SCO) was established on the basis of the Shanghai Five mechanism on June 15, 2001. China is always devoted to promoting good-neighborly friendship and cooperation between member states of the SCO, pushing forward the development of the Organization's practical cooperation and mechanism-building.

President Hu Jintao attended the meeting of the Council of Heads of States of the SCO upon invitation in June 2010. From the long-term perspective of maintaining solidarity and stability and promoting cooperation and development in the region, he contacted all parties concerned. His visit effectively promoted the sustained, healthy and stable development of the SCO and deepened China's mutually beneficial and wide-ranging cooperation with the SCO's member states and observer states.

China and the BRICS

BRIC refers to the countries of Brazil, Russia, India and China. It was first used by Goldman Sachs in 2001. Now, the group is referred to as BRICS after South Africa joined as a full member.

The second BRIC summit took place in Brazil in April 2010. In the joint statement after the summit, leaders of the four countries clarified their views and stands on issues like the global economic situation, and agreed on concrete measures of cooperation and coordination among them.

With the agreement of the other three, China, as the rotating president country of the BRIC cooperation mechanism, invited South Africa to join as a full member. The third BRICS summit took place in Sanya on the island of Hainan, China, in April 2011, with South Africa participating for the first time.

As major emerging economies, the BRICS countries encompass 27% of the world's land coverage and 43% of the world's population. Following the rapid economic growth of the five countries, the international influence of the BRICS keeps increasing.

Power grid construction

Economy

After more than 30 years of reform and opening up, a socialist market economy has been basically established in China, and an omni-directional pattern of opening up which is wide-ranging, multi-level with priorities has taken shape. China's economy has thus made great strides. Guided by the Scientific Outlook on Development, China stresses comprehensive, coordinated and sustainable economic development. The government strengthens and improves its macro control, and as a result, China's economy was the first to recover after the global financial crisis beginning in 2008. The 12th Five-year Plan for National Economy and Social Development, now being implemented, paints a grand picture for China.

Economic Development

China's economic development is guided by its "Five-year Plans." It implemented nine Five-year Plans from 1953 to 2000, laying a solid foundation for development. The 10th and 11th Five-year Plans (2001-2005 and 2006-2010) were remarkably successful in spurring China to enter the ranks of the world's strongest economies. Now the country is undertaking its 12th Five-year Plan (2011-2015).

Despite the global financial crisis, China's economy has maintained a growth rate of over 8% on average. Its GDP had reached No. 2 in the world by the second quarter of 2010.

With this rapid economic development, China's fiscal revenue has increased accordingly. By 2010 the national fiscal revenue had come to 8.308 trillion yuan, 1,340 times that of 1950. This greatly improves the government's macro control capability. Its opening-up policy has also helped greatly increase its foreign exchange reserves. Since 2006 China has led the world in the amount of its foreign exchange reserves.

With its exports hard hit by the global financial crisis, the

China is enhancing macro-control of real estate.

Scientific Outlook on Development

The Scientific Outlook on Development was put forward in July 2003. It takes into consideration China's national conditions in the primary stage of socialism, as well as its experience in development and that of other countries. It is an important strategic theory suited to the new stage of development in China, epitomizing the ideology of governance of Chinese leadership represented by Hu Jintao.

The Scientific Outlook on Development takes development as its essence, putting people first as its core, comprehensive, balanced and sustainable development as its basic requirement, and overall consideration as its fundamental approach.

That is to say, the development should be scientific, comprehensive, balanced and sustainable. This means to maintain a rational economic growth and oppose excessive growth; and try to raise the quality of economic growth: improving the industrial structure, consuming fewer resources and less energy, causing less harm to the ecology, stressing a knowledge-intensive approach and innovation, and gaining greater overall benefits.

China is promoting the restructuring of its textiles industry.

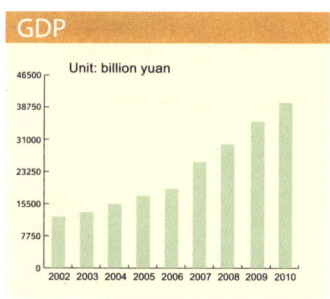

GDP

Unit: billion yuan

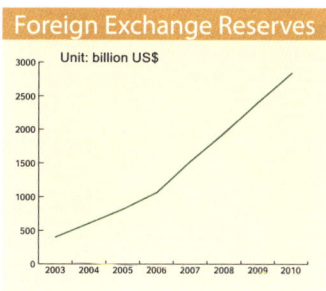

Foreign Exchange Reserves

Unit: billion US$

Chinese government, after closely evaluating the situation, took a series of measures to expand the domestic market to promote the stable and rapid growth of its economy. These measures included speeding up the construction of low-income housing, rural infrastructure, transportation infrastructure, medical, cultural and educational undertakings, ecological environment, and innovation and structural adjustment, and improving the income of rural and urban residents, encouraging technical upgrading in enterprises and increasing financial support for economic development.

China's huge population and relatively backward state of development determines that it is potentially one of the biggest and most promising economies in the world. It is still one of the developing countries, with its per capita GDP of US$3,800 putting it in 100th place in the world in this regard.

Economic System

A system of socialist market economy has taken shape in China. The market is playing an increasingly important role in allocating resources, and the macro-control system is being refined; the public and non-public sectors of the economy, including individually-owned businesses and private companies, compose a complementary economic structure. A relatively complete socialist market economy had been in place by 2010, which is expected to be accordingly mature by 2020.

Before 1978 China's economy was dominated by public sectors only, with state-owned and collective-owned enterprises representing 77.6% and 22.4%, respectively of all enterprises. The policy of reform and opening up has given wide scope to the development of various economic sectors. By now, almost all state-owned enterprises have adopted a corporate governance system. Their impact in terms of control, influence and leadership on the overall national economy has been constantly increasing. At present, the national economy features state-ownership alongside the new mixed economy and private economy. The state-owned economy dominates such fields as railways, civil aviation, posts and telecommunications, urban water, power and gas supplies, science and technology, education, national defense and finance. The private economy has grown swiftly, with many private firms moving away from traditional sectors like retail, foodstuffs, services, and repairs, while entering knowledge and hi-tech industries.

A large number of private businesses have created their own brands, winning extensive market opportunities. The picture shows a private company employee at work.

In 2008 26 enterprises from China's mainland ranked in the world's top 500, and non-public Chinese enterprises appeared on the list for the first time. Non-public enterprises have become the driving force in various industrial sectors, with the non-public economy accounting for 50% in 27 of the 40 industrial sectors, and more than 70% in some sectors. In terms of foreign trade, tax contribution and boosting employment, the non-public enterprises have overtaken the state-owned enterprises as the major contributor. Particular credit should be given to non-public enterprises after the outbreak of the international financial crisis in 2008. Though severely hit, they answered the national call, trying not to lay off workers, cut wages or hold back pay; rather, they safeguarded the legitimate rights of their employees and tided over the crisis together with the government, serving as an important force for maintaining social stability and pro-moting harmonious development.

Headquarters of China National Petroleum Corp

When proceeding with its economic restructuring, China will maintain economic growth while restructuring its economy to improve mechanisms and systems which aim to promote the transformation of the economic development pattern, combine government regulation with the role of the market to stimulate the internal power and vigor of economic development, integrate an innovative public service system with social development to perfect a social-security system aimed at improving the people's well-being, combine economic benefits with social equality to form an atmosphere conducive to social harmony and stability, and do a better job in opening up while boosting internal development to create a competitive edge in international cooperation and competition.

Economic Structure

Before 1978 China's economy was characterized by a weak agricultural foundation, and imbalanced light and heavy industries. But since it adopted the reform and opening-up policy, China has worked to give priority to the development of light industry, increase the import of high-end consumer goods, strengthen the basic industries and infrastructure, and develop tertiary industry, so as to balance, upgrade and optimize its economic structure.

These changes are manifested in the optimization of the primary, secondary and tertiary industries, and in this process the transformation from the dominat-

The employment of the tertiary industry is increasing steadily. The picture shows workers cleaning the outer walls of a building.

ing roles of industry and agriculture to the coordinated development of primary, secondary and tertiary industries is materialized. The internal structure of agriculture has been markedly improved, basically realizing the transformation from taking grain as the key link to the all-around development of agriculture, forestry, animal husbandry and fisheries. The industrial structure has been markedly upgraded, and it has basically achieved the transformation from being low-tech, labor intensive and simple to being diversified, and labor- and tech-intensive.

Great strides have been made in the strategic adjustment of the national economy, and the transformation from domination by the public sector to the development of various forms of ownership has been basically accomplished. Urbanization is speeding up, the gap between urban and rural areas has been gradually bridged, and their coordinated development is being realized. Regional development is more coordinated, with economic growth gravitating from the east coast toward the integrated development of the east, west and central regions. The distribution structure has been basically adjusted, realizing the transformation from prioritizing equalitarianism and lacking income channels to the coexistence of distribution according to one's work and distribution according to one's capital and technology.

Over the 30 years since China adopted the reform and opening-up policy, the irrational structure besetting its economic development has been improved greatly. At present, China sticks to structural adjustment, doing its utmost to solve the uneven development between regions, and between urban and rural areas through constantly upgrading its industrial structure, expanding the scope for the economic development of the next stage.

From Opening Up Coastal Areas to All-around Opening Up

In 1978 when China began its economic restructuring, it also implemented a policy of gradual opening up. Since 1980 it has established five special economic zones along its coast, opened up 14 coastal cities in addition to a group of border cities and all provincial and regional capital cities, and set up bonded zones, state economic and technological development zones and new- and hi-tech industrial development zones. The number of places opening up to the outside world kept increasing, with economic zones, coastal cities, coastal economic zones, inland cities and those on big rivers, and border cities. These places, with different preferential policies, serve as windows with a radiating influence on inland areas, for developing an export-oriented economy, generating foreign exchange earnings through exports, and importing advanced technologies. Thus a wide-ranging, multi-layer, focused pattern of opening up basically took shape.

On December 11, 2001 China officially joined the World Trade Organization (WTO), entering a new era of all-around opening up. The Chinese government, as promised, has changed the policy of opening up in certain areas to opening up in every possible area, opening sectors from traditional goods to services, and making market access more legitimate, transparent and standard. China has been thus fully integrated into the world economy, opening its market, economy and society. In the economic sector it promotes the free flow of goods, services and

Weihai, an open city in coastal Shandong Province

McDonald's and KFC fast food chain restaurants have spread rapidly in China.

factors of production across borders and optimizes the resource distribution according to the law of the market, so as to internationalize production and consumption, liberalize trade and investment, and deregulate and internalize the economic system. In addition, China conforms to the trend of economic globalization, persists in participating in the international economic and political order and international organizations within a broader scope and at a higher level, and actively plays its role in these areas. In terms of cooperation, China cooperates with both developing and developed countries, big and small; promotes South-South cooperation, and South-North cooperation; propels economic, trade, technical and security cooperation; and improves the competitiveness of domestic enterprises and industries in participating in the international market and fending off external shocks and risks.

Utilizing Foreign Capital

China utilizes foreign capital mainly through three channels: 1) foreign loans, in the forms of loans from foreign governments, international financial institutions and foreign commercial banks, export credits, and issuance of bonds overseas; 2) direct foreign investment – Chinese-foreign equity joint ventures, Chinese-foreign cooperative joint ventures, wholly foreign-owned enterprises and Chinese-foreign cooperative development projects; and 3) other foreign investment, by way of international leasing, compensation trade, processing and as-

TESCO debuted in Fuzhou in May 2011.

sembly, and issuance of stocks overseas. Over the past 30 years or so, China's utilization of foreign capital has kept its momentum, with foreign direct investment as the major form.

Jianghuai cars awaiting shipment to Africa at the port of Lianyungang

Since the 1980s the NPC and the State Council have promulgated over 500 foreign-related laws and regulations, providing a legal basis and guarantee for foreign investment in China. To this day, China has basically finished revision of foreign-related laws and regulations according to its commitments to and the rules of the WTO. At present, businessmen from about 200 countries and regions have come to China to invest, with the number of foreign-invested enterprises coming close to 600,000; international consortiums and transnational corporations favor the Chinese market too, and the top 500 large transnational companies have almost all invested in China, which has been hailed by world investors and financial sectors as one of the countries with best investment environment and potential.

Foreign trade

In terms of volume of foreign trade, China ranked No. 3 in the world in 2004, from No. 27 in 1978, No. 16 in 1990, and No.8 in 2000. In 2010 the volume of China's foreign trade totaled US$2,972.8 billion, an increase of 34.7% over the previous year. At present, there are altogether 230 countries and regions doing business with China's mainland, and its 10 largest trading partners are: the EU, the US, Japan, the ASEAN, China's Hong Kong Special Administrative Region, the ROK, China's Taiwan Province, India, Australia and Russia.

On July 1, 2004 China began to implement the newly revised Foreign Trade

Tariff Cut

Following China's entry into the WTO, its overall tariff level decreased to 9.8% in 2010 from 15.6% in 2000.

A free trade zone refers to an area that covers every aspect of tariff of the parties concerned as designated in agreements signed by two or more countries or regions and based on most-favored-nation status. In this area markets are further opened, tariff and non-tariff barriers are gradually abolished, market entry standards in service sectors are improved, and trade and investment are liberalized.

In recent years, the Chinese government has guided and promoted the process of regional cooperation, and accelerated the implementation of free trade zone strategy. By 2010, the Chinese mainland had forged closer trade partnerships with Hong Kong and Macao, signed free trade zone agreements with the ASEAN, Pakistan, Chile, New Zealand, Singapore, Peru and Costa Rica, and the Asia-Pacific Trade Agreement; negotiations with Australia, the Gulf Cooperation Council and the Southern African Customs Union on free trade zones are under way; and proposals for building free trade zones in Japan, the ROK, India and Switzerland are being studied.

Law. This law transformed the system of examination and approval for foreign trade into a registration system. It has clear provisions on the import and export of goods and technology, international trade in services, foreign-trade controls and related protection of intellectual property rights, etc., so as to accelerate the development of foreign trade.

Overseas Investment

China is emerging as a major investor worldwide. Its direct foreign investment is worth over US$280 billion in over 160 countries and regions, involving export trade, catering and simple processing to marketing networks, shipping logistics, resource exploration, manufacturing and design development. Transnational mergers and acquisitions is the major form of China's foreign investment.

The Second China Overseas Investment Fair opening in Beijing on November 2, 2010

Some large enterprises and groups have become multinationals with relatively strong international competitiveness, through specialized, intensive and scaled transnational management, widening of resource configuration and strengthening of capability to participate in overseas economic cooperation. Such group companies include China Petrochemical Company (Sinopec Group), State Grid Corporation of China and China National Petroleum Corporation (CNPC).

Coordinated Development of All Regions and Comprehensive Reform

The reform and opening-up policy, starting in 1978, has brought about great changes to and promoted the development of the eastern region of China.

"Develop the West"

In 2000 China launched its "Develop the West" campaign. The western region includes Gansu, Guizhou, Qinghai, Shaanxi, Sichuan and Yunnan provinces, the Tibet, Xinjiang Uyghur, Guangxi Zhuang, Inner Mongolia and Ningxia Hui autonomous regions, and Chongqing Municipality. It accounts for over 70% of China's total land area and nearly 30% of its total population.

Xi'an Economic and Technological Development Zone, Shaanxi Province

Western China, bordering on 13 countries, is rich in land resources and mineral reserves. Hence it is believed to be the next golden area for opening up, after the east coast. Boosted by preferential policies aimed at absorbing foreign investment, the western region has become attractive for foreign investors in the fields of logistics, IT, commerce, finance, security and trade.

"Revitalize the Northeast"

In 2003 the CPC Central Committee and the State Council put forward the "strategy to revitalize the old industrial bases in northeast China." Before 1978, when China introduced its reform and opening-up policy, northeast China was the country's most important industrial base and most developed area. After 1978 its economic development lagged far behind the national average. Measures such as social security and VAT reform, exemption from enterprise taxes in arrears, and policy-mandated bankruptcy of state-owned enterprises helped solve the deep-rooted institutional and structural problems, revealing its great potential for development. The northeast region has thus become again the most important base for commodity grain production, forestry, energy and raw materials, and the machinery and pharmaceuticals industries.

A coastal economic belt is facilitating the rejuvenation of Liaoning Province.

"Rise of Central China"

In 2004, in order to promote the rapid economic development of the six provinces (Shanxi, Jiangxi, Henan, Hubei, Hunan and Anhui) in central China, China put forward the strategy of "Rise of Central China." With only 10.7% of China's total land area but being home to 28.1% of the national population, this region creates 19.5% of the national GDP. As it is the breadbasket and important market with a big population, central China is an economic hub. The "Rise of

Highway-Railway Bridge over the Yellow River near Zhengzhou, Henan Province

Central China" strategy aims to improve the grain production capability in this area, cultivate bases for coal and quality raw materials production and construct an integrated traffic system.

"Reform Pilot Zones"

While implementing a series of strategies encouraging the eastern region to develop first, developing the west, revitalizing the old industrial bases in the northeast and promoting the rise of central China, China also set up some "state pilot zones for overall reform" to further explore how to build a harmonious society, innovate regional development mode, and improve regional and national competitiveness.

Different from the "special economic zones" designated in Shenzhen and other places after 1978, these state pilot zones for overall reform are set up to conduct comprehensive reform in some typical areas so as to provide new experience and thoughts for the reforms in economic, political and cultural systems across the country.

State Pilot Zones for Overall Reform

By the end of 2010 the State Council had ratified 10 state-level pilot zones for overall reforms, including the ones in the Shanghai Pudong New Area, Tianjin Binhai New Area and Shenzhen; for coordinated reform of rural and urban areas in Chongqing and Chengdu; for building a resource-saving and environment-friendly society in Wuhan and the Changsha-Zhuzhou-Xiangtan conurbation; for new industrialization in Shenyang; for transformation of the resource-based economy in Shanxi Province; and for international trade in Yiwu.

The 12th Five-year Plan

The 12th Five-year Plan for National Economy and Social Development, now being implemented, paints a grand picture for China's economic and social development, and puts forward the major targets for this period (2011-2015).

Major Indicators of Economic and Social Development During the 12th Five-year Plan Period

Indicators		2010	2015	Average Annual Growth Rate (%)	Note
Economic Growth					
GDP (trillion yuan)		39.8	55.8	7	Anticipated
Ratio of Added Value of Service Industry (%)		43	47	[4]	Anticipated
Urbanization Rate (%)		47.5	51.5	[4]	Anticipated
Science & Education					
Consolidation Rate of Nine-year Compulsory Education (%)		89.7	93	[3.3]	Obligatory
High School Gross Enrollment Rate (%)		82.5	87	[4.5]	Anticipated
Ratio of R&D Expenditure in GDP (%)		1.75	2.2	[0.45]	Anticipated
Patent Ownership (thousand people)		17	33	[1.6]	Anticipated
Resources and Environment					
Total Cultivated Land (million ha)		121.2	121.2	[0]	Obligatory
Reduction of Water Consumption per-unit Industrial Added Value (%)				[30]	Obligatory
Efficient Utilization Coefficient of Agricultural Irrigation Water		0.5	0.53	[0.03]	Anticipated
Ratio of Non-fossil Energy in Primary Energy Consumption (%)		83	11.4	[3.1]	Obligatory
Reduction of Energy Consumption per-unit GDP (%)				[16]	Obligatory
Reduction of CO_2 per-unit GDP (%)				[17]	Obligatory
Reduction of CO_2 per-unit GDP (%)	Reduction of Major Pollutant Emission (%)			[8]	Obligatory
	COD			[8]	
	SO_2			[10]	
	oxyhydrogen			[10]	
hydroxide Forest Growth(%)	Forest Coverage	20.36	21.66	[1.3]	Obligatory
	Forest Reserves (billion m^3)	13.7	14.3	[6]	
Quality of Life					
Per-capita Disposable Income of Urban Residents (yuan)		19109	>26810	>7	Anticipated
Per-capita Net Income of Rural Residents (yuan)		5919	>8310	>7	Anticipated
Registered Urban Unemployment Rate (%)		4.1	<5		Anticipated
Newly Increased Urban Employment in 5 Years (million people)				[4500]	Anticipated
Urban Population Covered by Basic Pension (million people)		257	357	[1]	Obligatory
Coverage of Urban & Rural Basic Medical Insurances (%)				[3]	Obligatory
Housing Projects for Low-income Urban Families (thousand suits)				[3600]	Obligatory
Total Population (billion people)		1.34	<1.39	<7.2‰	Obligatory
Life Expectancy (years old)		73.5	74.5	[1]	Anticipated

Note: ① figures for GDP and income of rural and urban residents are at 2010 prices, and the growth rate is based on comparable prices; ② those in [] are cumulative figures of five years; ③ the coverage of urban and rural basic medical insurances refers to urban workers and non-working urban residents covered by basic medical insurances and those covered by new rural cooperative medical care system; ④ the income increase of rural and urban residents should be no less than the designated goal of GDP growth, and try to be consistent with economic growth.

Terraced farmland

Agriculture

With only 7% of the world's cultivated land, China successfully feeds one fifth of the world's population.

Given a rural population of 900 million, the Chinese government has all along set as its top priority the solving of the issues related to agriculture, rural areas and farmers. Since the introduction of the reform and opening-up policy, China has established a two-tier management system that integrates unified and separated management on the basis of household contract management, opened up the markets for agricultural products in an all-round way and given agricultural tax exemptions and direct subsidies to farmers, initially shaping a rural economic system suited to the national conditions and geared to the needs of developing productivity. China has steadily increased grain yields and added variety to the supply of agricultural products, and has greatly improved rural incomes and made remarkable achievements in poverty alleviation. The government has gradually set up and expanded the social security system and a new cooperative medical system in rural areas, and popularized nine-year compulsory education. Township enterprises and small towns have developed rapidly, while rural markets have flourished, and a large rural labor force has found non-agricultural employment, with millions of rural migrant workers becoming an important part of China's industrial workforce. Industrialization, urbanization, modernization and social undertakings have accelerated in rural areas.

China leads the world in the outputs of grain, cotton, oil-bearing crops, fruit, meat, eggs, aquatic products and vegetables. With the continuous growth in the import and export trade of agricultural products, aquatic products, vegetables and fruit have become competitive farm products with a net export.

Expanding the scale of agricultural industrialization and promoting the all-round modernization of agriculture have been important factors in enhancing agricultural competitiveness in recent years. Now a pattern has been formed, spearheaded by some 600 national key enterprises, over 2,000 provincial key enterprises and a number of agencies connecting farmers with production bases. So far, a large number of villages and towns in east China have become specialized in export-oriented production, and many specializing in crop cultivation and stock breeding in central and western regions.

In 2008 the Third Plenary Session of the 17th CPC Central Committee adopted the Decision on Major Issues Concerning the Advancement of Rural Reform and Development, which expounded on how to promote rural reform and development in the new situation. It made it clear that the current land contract relations should be maintained for a long time to come; the contractual right of land can be transferred in forms of sub-contracting, leasing and joint-stock cooperation according

Work of Agriculture, Rural Areas and Farmers: Still Focus of the No.1 Document

In recent years the No. 1 Document released by the CPC Central Committee and the State Council at the beginning of the year has continuously focused on the "Three Rural Issues":

In 2003 the experimental reform of rural taxes and administrative charges went into full swing. In 2004 increase of rural incomes was promoted. In 2005 efforts were stepped up to further improve overall agricultural production. In 2006 the construction of a new socialist countryside was promoted. In 2007 modern agriculture was developed and the construction of a new socialist countryside continued. In 2008 the building of agricultural infrastructure was promoted, and farmers' income increased. In 2009 the steady development of agriculture was promoted, along with a continuous increase in farmers' incomes. In 2010 efforts were intensified to balance rural and urban development, and solidify the basis for the development of agriculture and the rural areas as a whole. In 2011 the development and reform of water conservancy is expedited.

Harvest season

to law and on a voluntary and compensatory basis so as to develop moderate-scale operations. The central authorities also decided to abolish the agricultural tax, provide support for migrant workers returning home in terms of employment, training and starting businesses, ensure all qualified low-income villagers have access to the rural subsistence allowance system, and let all farmers enjoy the benefits of the social security system of medical and pension insurance.

Thanks to a series of pro-rural policies, China's agriculture and rural economy have kept sustained and stable development in spite of drastic natural disasters such as floods, droughts and hailstones. Both the total and per-ha grain yield have reached historical highs, and edible oil production is recovering after decreasing for eight consecutive years. Livestock, aquaculture, and fruit and vegetable growing are improving and enriching the market supply. In 2010 the per capita income of farmers totaled 5,919 yuan, an increase of 14.9% over the previous year, which was a greater increase than that of urban residents for the first time since 1998.

In 2011 the No. 1 Document released by the central authorities again focused on the issues related to agriculture, farmers and rural areas, attaching great importance to the construction of water conservancy projects and reform in this regard.

Industry

Since the adoption of the reform and opening-up policy, China's industry has realized leapfrog development, and reached a new high in overall economic strength and restructuring efforts, laying a solid foundation for the country's transition to a manufacturing power.

The 16th National Congress of the CPC proposed the path of "new industrialization," and its 17th National Congress further stressed the integration of informatization and industriali-

"Ocean Petroleum 981," jointly built by China National Offshore Oil Corp. and China State Shipbuilding Corp., is the world's most advanced sixth-generation deepwater semi-submersible drilling platform.

Shenyang Economic Zone has been approved as a state-level new-type industrialization pilot reform zone.

zation, unswervingly following the path of new industrialization with Chinese characteristics, featuring scientific and technological content, good economic returns, low resource consumption and little environmental pollution, together with a full display of its advantages in human resources. At present, a comprehensive and complete modern industry system and communications industry has been set up in China. It includes a rich support chain and complete industry system encompassing fields such as raw materials and energy, equipment, consumption, science and technology for national defense and electronic information, and industrial goods in various key fields with advanced production capability and world-standard output.

Raw Materials Industry

In 1996 China's steel output exceeded 100 million tons for the first time, making the country the largest steel producer in the world, and by 2005 it had become a net importer of steel products. In chemical engineering, China has earmarked three regions to specialize in phosphate fertilizer production in Yunnan, Guizhou and Hubei, and launched potash projects in Qinghai and Xinjiang each with a

From "Made in China" to "Created by China"

At present, China's new and hi-tech industry is developing rapidly, ranking third in terms of scale in the world, and its export volume has reached the world's second place, becoming the new growth point in its industrial and economic development.

As a new term, "created by China" is taking the place of "made in China" and being gradually recognized the world over. It conveys the concept of high-level creative brain work rather than simple manual labor.

Through assimilating and re-innovating the technologies introduced, large-scale technical upgrading and with the aid of foreign investment, industrial enterprises are improving their production capability, making breakthroughs in a group of key projects and producing more domestically-made key equipment. Technical innovations are improved constantly and industrial technological upgrading is fruitful. Innovation capacity building is making headway in the national engineering laboratories, national engineering research centers, technical centers of enterprises, etc. Efforts have been made to protect intellectual property rights and a standardized management system has been established.

Haizhou strip mine in Fuxin, Liaoning Province

production capacity of one million tons. All this has made China a big producer and consumer of petrochemicals, with the output of many of its products ranking top in the world. China is the world's largest producer, user and exporter of rare earth. Since 2001 the output of China's 10 nonferrous metals has ranked first in the world, its foreign trade volume increased year by year, the amount of energy consumed per unit of GDP dropped markedly, and overseas resource exploitation made breakthroughs. In innovations in the building materials industry, China's major products, technology and equipment have reached or come close to advanced international level. China has made remarkable achievements in energy conservation and emission reduction, and also made steady progress in exploring the development pattern of a cyclical economy.

Equipment Industry

Over the past decade, China has made significant progress in key aspects of the equipment industry, such as output, technology, mastery and innovation of key technologies, management and global competitiveness. Particularly by relying on state key projects, achievements have been made in the rejuvenation of the equipment industry, and high-end equipment manufacturing has also taken shape.

Restructuring and Rejuvenating 10 Industries

To reverse the ill effects of the global financial crisis on economic development, and realize the goal of macro economic development, the State Council approved successively in January and February 2010 the rejuvenation programs for 10 industries: automobiles, iron and steel, equipment manufacturing, textiles, shipping, electronic information, light industry, petrochemicals, nonferrous metals and logistics.

So far, these programs are playing a marked role in coping with the repercussions of the financial crisis and sustaining fast yet steady economic growth, while looking to the future to solve step by step existing structural contradictions, forming new economic growth points and greatly improving the level of industrial development.

A workshop of Yuandong Cable Co., Ltd in Wuxi, Jiangsu Province

Workers checking a seamless steel tube at an iron and steel plant in Anhui Province

As one of the largest industries in China, the number of related enterprises, staff, value of output, and taxes account for 20% to 25% of all industries nation-wide. About 80% of the production capacity in various industries is guaranteed by the support of equipment made in China. As its industrial added value takes up 5.2% of the GDP, these items have become pillar products in China's foreign trade, with an export volume accounting for 21.5% of the nation's total.

Consumer Goods Industry

In the past 30 years, the aggregate export value of China's textile products exceeded US$2 trillion. The output of over 100 products such as bicycles, sewing machines, batteries and beer ranked top in the world. Household appliances, leather goods, furniture, down products, porcelain and bicycles take up over 50% of the international market.

Chinese weaving enjoys a worldwide reputation. Its output of chemical fiber, yarn, cloth, wool fabric, silk and clothing ranks top in the world. Its production of cotton accounts for a quarter of the world's total, and that of chemical fiber half of the world's total. The textile industry is one of China's most competitive industries. Large textile enterprises employ 20 million workers, thereby contributing greatly to job creation.

Aeronautics

As the fifth country to independently develop and launch man-made satellites and the third to master satellite recovery technology, China is in the world's front ranks in such important technological fields as satellite recovery, carrying of multiple satellites on one rocket, rocket technology, and testing and operation of static-orbit satellites. Great achievements have been made in the manufacturing and application of remote-sensing and communication satellites, and manned space-craft. These achievements serve all aspects of the national economy.

Shenzhou-V was the first manned spacecraft independently developed by China. Shenzhou-VII, launched in 2008, carried three astronauts, one of whom performed China's maiden spacewalk, making China the third country to master the key technology for putting humans in space. The successful launch of the Chang'e-1 and Chang'e-2 satellites in 2007 and 2010, respectively, made China the fifth country to launch lunar orbiters into space. The images of the moon's surface thus recovered were the most complete and vivid up to that time.

So far, China has developed 12 models of the Long March carrier rocket series, and set up three launching sites in Jiuquan, Xichang and Taiyuan. Aerospace technology in China has evolved into a space research system and production and experimental base devoted to the development of carrier rockets and application satellites guided by high technology.

China's aeronautics sector is working to launch space labs, accomplish unmanned and manned docking, and construct a space station. China is willing to conduct more extensive international cooperation with each friendly state so as to better utilize outer space for the benefit of mankind.

Information Industry

The information industry has become the mainstay of China's industry. In 2010 the added value of the information industry accounted for 10% of the GDP, with the production of computer screens, cell phones and notebook computers ranking top in the world. The output value, sales and profits of China's electronics and communications equipment manufacturing industry have surpassed those of traditional industries, ranking top among all industries and making the biggest contribution to the growth of the national economy.

By 2010 the number of telephone subscribers in China had reached 1.15 billion, including 300 million of fixed-line subscribers and 850 million of mobile phone users, and that of netizens stood at 440 million, all ranking top in the world. Besides, the number of 3G (third-

3G cell phone

Zhongguancun in Beijing, nicknamed "China's Silicon Valley," where a large number of hi-tech enterprises are situated

generation) users exceeded 40 million. In 2011 3G mobile services will cover all cities at prefectural level, and most counties, townships, major expressways and scenic spots.

The government is making efforts to improve the fiber-optic broadband network, focusing on the access to each household. China Telecom has started 8M access bandwidth in all cities; each township has access capacity of 2M, and 100m fiber-optic broadband access is being installed in some large cities. So far, China has a total of 10 million fiber-optic broadband subscribers, among whom 100,000 are home users.

The Beidou satellite navigation system is a global satellite navigation system that China has independently developed. On April 10, 2011, China successfully sent the eighth satellite into orbit. The Beidou system is expected to cover the Asia-Pacific region by 2012, and the entire world by 2020.

Service Industries

At present, the proportion of the three types of industry in China's GDP is as follows: primary industry 10% to 20%, secondary industry 45% to 50%, and tertiary industry 40%.

The rapid development of the service industries, particularly modern types of such industries, is the salient feature in the process of industrial restructuring.

The catering industry is developing rapidly in China. The picture shows a street full of prosperous eateries.

Significant development has been achieved in the traditional service sectors such as transportation, wholesale and retail and catering, playing an important role in creating jobs and benefiting the general public. To adapt to the needs of industrialization, urbanization, deregulation of the market, informatization, and internationalization, modern service sectors, including finance, insurance, real estate, consultancy, e-commerce, modern logistics and tourism, are making great strides, improving the overall quality of China's tertiary industry.

China lags behind the developed countries whose proportion of service industries in their GDP standing at 70% to 80%. So it is trying to change the over-reliance of its economic growth on secondary industry, putting the strategic focus on the service industries to promote the upgrading of industrial restructuring. For this purpose, it creates policies and an institutional environment conducive to the service industries, explores new areas and sectors, and encourages the chain operation. The goal is to raise the proportion in the GDP of the service industries to 55% by 2015.

Transportation

China's transportation network, and passenger and freight volume keep increasing rapidly. In 2010 the total length of land, sea and air transportation stood at 7.0427 million km, passenger volume reached 32.791 billion, and the cargo turnover stood at 32.03 billion tons.

◇Highways

Highways are China's key infrastructure. By the end of 2010, the total length of highways reached 3.984 million km, including a grid of five north-south and seven east-west arteries which was completed 13 years ahead of schedule, and eight inter-provincial highways for the development of the western region. The density of roads across the country had reached 40.2 km per 100 square km.

According to the National Expressway Network Plan, China will build an expressway system connecting all provincial capitals with Beijing and each other, linking major cities as well as important counties. The plan calls for a grid of five radiating, two north-south and seven east-west arteries, of which work on 74,100 km is already under way, accounting for 95% of the total length and ranking second in the world. In the past five years alone, the length of the newly built expressways was equivalent to 44.5% of the total. It is predicted that in the next five years the total length of China's expressways will reach 100,000 km, ranking top in the world.

New Energy Autos

In 2009 China became the world's biggest auto seller. Its auto industry is accordingly facing a rare opportunity for restructuring. The government encourages new energy autos represented by electric motor vehicles, supports the improvement of the competitiveness of core components for traditional and new energy cars, and encourages auto exports, mergers and acquisitions abroad. All departments concerned have promulgated and are speeding up their implementation of supportive policies, with the focus on electric motor vehicles.

The goal by 2020 is to build China into a powerful auto maker, getting its traditional cars recognized around the world, with its autos and components export taking up over 10% of world auto trade; getting its new energy autos a solid industry dominating the world market, with five million new energy autos running on the road.

Electric taxis being charged in Yanqing County, Beijing

Sketch Map of Highway Network

Urumqi

Lhasa

Nanning Guangzhou
          Hong Kong
    Macao
  Haikou

South China Sea Is.

——	Expressways
——	National highways
----	Provincial highways

Harbin

Changchun

Shenyang

Hohhot

Beijing

Tianjin

Yinchuan

Taiyuan

Shijiazhuang

Jinan

Xining

Lanzhou

Zhengzhou

Xi'an

Nanjing

Shanghai

Hefei

Chengdu

Wuhan

Hangzhou

Chongqing

Nanchang

Changsha

Guiyang

Fuzhou

Taibei

ning

Nanning

Guangzhou

Macao

Hong Kong

Haikou

At the end of 2010 there were 91,000 km of railway track, the second biggest such network in the world, including 42,000 km of electrified track, second only to Russia.

The Qinghai-Tibet railway was completed and opened to traffic in 2006. It is the highest and longest plateau railway and has the highest speed (100 km/h) of travel through permafrost areas. Its applied engineering techniques reach the advanced international standard, promoting world progress in this regard. In 2010 the Datong-Qinhuangdao Railway broke the world freight capacity record, with its annual freight load exceeding 400 million tons. In the same year the Yichang-Wanzhou Railway, which was most difficult and most expensive to build in China, was opened to traffic. Out of the line's total 377 km length, 288 km is over bridges or through tunnels.

The new generation of CRH (China Railway High-speed) trains made by China has set a world record speed of 486.1 km/h. The Beijing-Shanghai High-speed Railway, which

Railway Transport Speeds

- 120 km/h and above
- 160 km/h and above
- 200 km/h and above
- 250 km/h and above

Harbin

Changchun

Shenyang

Hohhot

Beijing

Tianjin

Yinchuan

Taiyuan

Shijiazhuang

Xining

Jinan

Lanzhou

Xi'an

Zhengzhou

Hefei

Nanjing

Shanghai

Chengdu

Wuhan

Hangzhou

Chongqing

Changsha

Nanchang

Guiyang

Fuzhou

Taibei

Kunming

Nanning

Guangzhou

Macao

Hong Kong

Haikou

The construction of the Qinghai-Tibet Railway hasn't affected the water quality of Tsonag Lake.

opened to traffic in 2011, is 1,302 km long, and designed for a maximum speed of 380 km/h. It connects three municipalities and four provinces in the Bohai Economic Rim and the Yangtze River Delta, covering 11 cities each with a population of over one million and with their GDP making up 43.3% of the national total.

By the end of 2010 China had 8,358 km of high-speed railways in operation, ranking first in the world. There are more than 10,000 km under construction at the moment. This makes China the country with the fastest-expanding high-speed railways, most complete railway engineering technologies, best integration capacity, longest operating distance, fastest speed and largest scale.

A train passes through Zaozhuang Station in Shandong Province, on the Beijing-Shanghai High-speed Railway

◇ Light Rail Transit

In recent years, the government has increased its investment in the construction of LRT (light rail transit) to lessen the pressure on urban transport. LRT systems have been put into use in large cities like Beijing, Tianjin, Shanghai, Chongqing, Guangzhou, Dalian and Nanjing. It is estimated that a total of 2,000 km of light rail lines will be in operation by 2020, and 4,500 km by 2050. By then, these LRTs will be integrated with subways, suburban railways and other rail systems, to form a rapid traffic system, taking 50% to 80% of the total load of public traffic in cities.

◇ Ports

During the 11th Five-year Plan period, China invested more than 350 billion yuan in the construction of its coastal ports, as well as along the arteries of the Yangtze and Pearl rivers, and the Beijing-Hangzhou Grand Canal. In 2010 the cargo-handling capacity of large ports stood at 8.02 billion tons, and Chinese ports' freight volume has maintained the first position in the world for six successive years. Remarkable achievements in port building have become the engine to boost harbor industry and regional economic development.

The Port of Ningbo

Among the 16 ports with freight volume exceeding 100 million tons a year, those of Shanghai, Shenzhen, Qingdao, Tianjin, Guangzhou, Xiamen, Ningbo and Dalian are listed among the world's top 50 container ports. The Port of Shanghai holds the first position in the world in this regard. The size of China's merchant fleet ranks fourth in the world, and its shipbuilding tonnage accounts for 25% of the world's shipbuilding market, ranking first in the world.

Sketch Map of River and Sea Ports

Guangzhou
Shantou
Shenzhen
Beihai
Hong Kong
Gaoxiong
Zhanjiang
Dongfang
Haikou
Sanya

South China Sea Is.

Heilong River

Heihe

Songhua River

Harbin

Qinhuangdao

Beijing ★

Tianjin

Dalian

Yantai

Grand Canal

Yellow River

Qingdao

Jining

Rizhao

Lianyungang

Yangzhou

Nantong

Nanjing

Shanghai

Yangtze River

Wuhu

Suzhou

Chongqing

Wuhan

Hangzhou

Ningbo

Jiujiang

Wenzhou

Fuzhou

Quanzhou

Jilong

Xiamen

Wuzhou

Guangzhou

Shantou

Gaoxiong

Pearl River

Shenzhen

Beihai

Hong Kong

Zhanjiang

Haikou

Dongfang

Sanya

— Navigable rivers
● Major coastal ports
● Major river ports

Note: not including Hong Kong, Macao and Taiwan Province.

By the end of 2010 China's civil aviation routes covered 2.765 million km, and there were 175 airports nationwide, forming a well functioning airport network of adequate scale. They cover an area which creates 91% of the nation's aggregate GDP and is home to 76% of the country's total population. The volume of passenger traffic at Beijing's Capital Airport and that of freight traffic at Shanghai's Pudong Airport rank second and third, respectively, in the world.

China has the second biggest air transport system in the world. In 2010 China had 1,604 civil aircraft, and its volume of passenger traffic reached 270 million persons a year.

Chinese civil airlines are mainly state-run, including Air China, Southern Airlines, China Eastern Airlines and Hainan Airlines. Government backing is being given to private and Sino-foreign jointly owned airlines, showing good momentum for development.

Finance and Insurance
◇ Financial System

China has basically formed a financial system under the regulation, control and supervision of the central bank, with state banks as the mainstay, featuring the separation of policy-related banks and commercial banks, and the cooperation of various financial institutions with mutually complementary functions.

The People's Bank of China (PBOC) no longer handles credit and savings business, but exercises a central bank's functions and powers. State-owned specialized banks are being set up one by one; insurance companies are being established and expanding their operations both at home and abroad; shareholding banks and regional banks have begun to be reorganized; trust and investment institutions are mushrooming; leasing and finance companies, urban credit cooperatives, cooperative banks, securities companies, stock exchanges, credit evaluation companies, Sino-foreign joint-venture banks and foreign banks are all being introduced.

Beijing's Financial Street

The People's Bank of China

Billboards advertising foreign-funded banks in Shanghai

In this way, a modern financial system with specialized banks as the mainstay, the central bank as the core, and integrating bank-type with non-bank-type financial institutions, is being set up.

◇Banking

The banking industry is in the forefront of China's finance industry. China's banks at the present stage fall into three categories: central bank, commercial banks and policy-related banks. The PBOC exercises the power and function of the central bank, being responsible for making monetary policies, issuing currency and handling reserves of foreign exchange and gold. The Industrial and Commercial Bank of China (ICBC), Bank of China (BOC), Agricultural Bank of China (ABC) and Construction Bank of China (CBC) are state-owned commercial banks. The Agricultural Development Bank of China, China Development Bank and China Import and Export Bank, once policy-related banks, are in the process of changing into shareholding commercial banks.

Besides, China has over 100 urban commercial banks, more than 1,000 urban credit cooperatives and a large number of rural credit cooperatives. There are about 200 foreign financial institutions operating in China, 84 of which are allowed to handle transactions in China's currency, renminbi (RMB).

The reform of financial institutions has made breakthroughs. The BOC, the CBC, the ICBC and the ABC have been transformed into shareholding institutions, allowing them to be listed on the Hong Kong and Shanghai stock exchanges. The policy-related banks are also undergoing transformation to shareholding commercial banks. Through reform, the ownership and governance structure of financial institutions are being improved gradually; their management is undergoing a fundamental change; and their capital adequacy ratio, asset quality, profitability and risk control ability are markedly enhanced. The market value, profitability and capital savings of the four state-owned commercial banks rank among the top in the world, and in 2010 the ICBC was listed by *Forbes* magazine among the five most reputable companies in the world.

◇ Currency and Exchange Rates

The RMB is issued and controlled solely by the PBOC. RMB exchange rates are decided by the PBOC and announced by the State Administration of Foreign Exchange, the latter exercising the functions and powers of exchange control.

The RMB experienced the change from a single exchange rate, multiple exchange rate to single exchange rate again. Through the reform of the foreign-exchange system, China has synchronized the official foreign-exchange rate with the adjusted foreign-exchange rate of the RMB, adopted the bank exchange settlement system, set up a unified inter-bank foreign-exchange market, and included the foreign-exchange business of foreign-invested enterprises in the bank's exchange settlement system. On December 1, 1996 China formally accepted Article 8 of the Agreement on International Currencies and Funds, and realized RMB convertibility under current accounts ahead of schedule. In July 2005 China announced that it was adopting a floating exchange rate, and that the RMB would no longer be pegged to the US dollar. Since this reform, the RMB has gained 21% against the US dollar.

A bank teller counts dollar bills in Qionghai, Hainan Province.

China's exchange rate policy has been consistent and responsible, committed to the reform of the RMB exchange rate. China will adhere to three principles on

Overseas Operation of Chinese Commercial Banks

In 1980 China resumed its membership in the World Bank, and returned to the International Monetary Fund. In 1984 it started business contacts with the Bank for International Settlements; in 1985 it formally became a member of the African Development Bank, and in 1986 of the Asian Development Bank. At present, China's main commercial banks have set up over 60 overseas branches to develop international credit business.

currency policy: any change must be controlled, it must be on the government's own initiative and any shift must be gradual. Guided by these principles, China will improve its managed floating exchange rate system, give full play to the role of the market, increase the flexibility of the RMB exchange rate and maintain the currency's stability at an appropriate level.

China carries out bilateral currency exchanges with the ROK, Malaysia, Belarus, Indonesia and Argentina. By the end of 2010 China's foreign exchange reserves stood at US$ 2.8 trillion, and its share in the International Monetary Fund had risen to third place.

◇ Securities

In 1990 and 1991 China set up securities exchanges in Shanghai and Shenzhen, respectively. Since then, the Chinese stock market has matured, completing a journey that took many countries 100 years or more to navigate. The Chinese stock market has promoted the reform of state-owned enterprises and changes to their systems, and enabled a stable transition between the two systems. As for ordinary citizens, the stock market has joined bank deposits as the main channels for investment.

Today, a network system for securities exchange account settlement has been formed, with the Shanghai and Shenzhen exchanges as the powerhouses, radiating to all parts of the country. The technology has reached advanced international standards, with the realization of paperless trading. By early March 2011 there were 2,348 domestically listed companies, with a total market value of 26.88 trillion yuan.

Perusing
stock prices

◇ Insurance

The insurance industry in China was resumed in 1980, after 20 years of inertia. In 1981 the People's Insurance Company of China was transformed from a government department into a specialized company, with branches or sub-branches in every part of the country. The year 1988 witnessed the founding of the Ping An Insurance (Group) Company and the Pacific Insurance Company, both operating mainly in the coastal areas; and 2003 saw the establishment of the PICC Property and Casualty Company Ltd and China Life Insurance Company Ltd. The promulgation of the Insurance Law in 1995 and the establishment of the China Insurance Regulatory Commission in 1998 have provided a legal basis and specific rules for the smooth operation of the insurance market.

China's insurance industry is actively exploring the international market, setting up operations and representative offices in Southeast Asia, Europe and North America.

Tourism
◇ Tourism Market

In recent years China's tourism market has grown rapidly. Some 2.2 billion trips are made within China every year, and total tourism revenue exceeds one trillion

yuan. The tourism industry has created 11 million jobs, tourism added value accounts for over 4% of the national GDP, and tourist spending contributes over 10% to total consumption.

The Chinese on average make 1.5 trips abroad each year, and the country receives 50 million inbound tourists staying for over one night, the third most in the world. China has approved over 110 countries and regions as tourism destinations for Chinese citizens at their own expense, ranking fourth in the world in terms of outbound tourist numbers. In November 2007, the 17th general assembly of the World Tourism Organization unanimously approved the listing of Chinese as an official language of the organization, which predicts that by 2020 China will become the world's top tourist destination.

◇ Tourism Services

The rapid development of China's transport infrastructure has provided safe and convenient transportation for overseas and domestic tourists. Throughout China, great numbers of hotels have been constructed, renovated or expanded, to satisfy all levels of tourist requirements, and there are now more than 10,000

The Great Wall at Badaling, near Beijing

star-rated hotels. All large or medium-sized cities and scenic spots have hotels with full facilities and services.

China has about 20,000 travel agencies, 2,000 of which are capable of providing services for inbound tourists and 1,070 for outbound services. In 2003 the Chinese government allowed the establishment of foreign-controlled or foreign-invested travel agencies. The first wholly foreign-funded travel agency to enter China's tourism market was JALPAK International China Co. Ltd. The first overseas-controlled joint venture was TUI China Travel Company, in cooperation with the largest European travel group TUI and Martin Buese China Ltd, its Chinese partner being China Travel Service (CTS). So far, China has over 20 foreign-controlled or foreign-invested travel agencies.

The 17-arch Bridge at the Summer Palace, Beijing

Tourism Resources

China abounds in natural landscapes and places of cultural interest. By 2010 it had altogether 29 cultural sites, eight natural scenery sites, and four mixed sites on UNESCO's World Heritage List. It is the country with the most items on UNESCO's Intangible Cultural Heritage list.

China has 110 famous cultural cities each with a history of over 1,000 years, and 339 excellent tourism cities. It is made up of 56 ethnic groups, with diverse cultures and customs. In Yunnan, Guizhou, Sichuan, Guangxi, Hunan, Hubei, Gansu, Ningxia, Tibet, Inner Mongolia and Xinjiang, with large minority communities, it is possible to view a great variety of folk cultures and customs. Hainan will be built into a top tourism resort by 2020. The tropical island adopted the offshore duty-free policy as of April 20, 2011.

◇ Major Tourism Routes

Essential China Tour

Beijing, Shaanxi, Shanghai and Guangdong.

Great Wall Tour

From Beijing and Hebei to Ningxia and Gansu, visiting the better-preserved sections of the Great Wall.

Sea / Lake Holiday Tour

12 national tourist retreat areas, including Sanya in Hainan, Qingdao in Shandong, Dalian in Liaoning, Beihai in Guangxi, Putian and Wuyi Mountain in Fujian, and Kunming's Dianchi Lake.

Silk Road Tour

Urumqi, Xining, Yinchuan, Lanzhou and Xi'an, along the ancient Silk Road.

China Health and Fitness Tour

Shanghai, Jiangsu, Hebei and Shaanxi, experiencing traditional Chinese acupuncture and massage, and learning *taijiquan* (Chinese shadowboxing), *taijijian* sword and fitness *qigong*.

Religious Culture Tour

Mainly visiting renowned temples or monasteries, e.g., in Beijing, Shanxi, Anhui, Zhejiang, Sichuan, Hubei, Qinghai, and Tibet.

Central China Folk Customs Tour

Shanxi, Henan and Shandong, highlights of folk villages and scenic sites.

Ice and Snow Tour

Liaoning, Heilongjiang and Jilin, to appreciate the rime, ice lanterns and sculptures, as well as folk customs, and for skiing.

Southwest China Folk Customs Tour

Yunnan, Guizhou, Guangxi and Sichuan, highlighting minority folk customs, villages and scenic sites.

South China Riverside Village Tour

Hangzhou, Jiaxing and Shaoxing in Zhejiang Province, and Nanjing, Yangzhou, Wuxi and Suzhou in Jiangsu Province, experiencing local landscape and customs.

Three Gorges Tour

Along the Yangtze River to Chongqing, Sichuan, Hunan and Hubei, visiting renowned natural and cultural sites in the Three Gorges region.

Folk Customs Tour

Along the Yellow River to Qinghai, Gansu, Ningxia, Shanxi, Inner Mongolia, Henan and Shandong, visiting renowned natural and cultural sites.

Landscape Tour

Fujian, Guangxi, Anhui, Guizhou, Hunan, Jilin and Sichuan, visiting renowned natural and cultural sites.

The beach area in Sanya on Hainan Island is among the best in China.

Altai Pastureland, Xinjiang Uyghur Autonomous Region

Rime decorates trees in Jilin Province.

Zhouzhuang, a town built on water

Zhangjiajie scenery

Storks

Environmental Protection

Many places in China were densely wooded and had beautiful landscapes in the past, but due to such factors as large population and a backward economy, those places have seen vegetation deterioration, soil erosion and even desertification. In recent years, the Chinese government has attached great importance to the principle of prevention first, integrated treatment and promoting the work in an all-round way with breakthroughs in key areas, and has been transforming the past development mode which preferred economic growth to environmental protection into one focusing on economic growth in tandem with environmental protection.

China International Green Industry Expo

Laws and Systems for Environmental Protection

The Chinese Constitution specifies that "The state protects and improves the environment in which people live and the ecological environment. It prevents and controls pollution and other public hazards." Environmental protection has been a basic national policy since the 1980s. The first Environmental Protection Law was issued in 1989. Over the past two decades and more, laws and regulations, including the Energy Conservation Law, Renewable Energy Law and Circular Economy Promotion Law, have been promulgated to refine the environmental protection legal system. Furthermore, a central and local system of environmental protection standards has also been set up across the country. In 2008 the State Environmental Protection Administration was upgraded to the Ministry of Environmental Protection.

China has adopted an environmental management system with governments at all levels being accountable for local environmental quality, competent departments exercising supervision, and related departments administering in accordance with the law. A system of inter-ministerial joint meetings for environmental protection has been in place, and representative offices for regional environmental protection supervision have been set up to enhance coordination and cooperation between departments and regions.

New Changes in Environmental Protection

Traditional environmental protection methods are being transformed in the process of the gradual perfection of relevant legal system. The earlier end-of-pipe treatment system and remedial management modes are being transformed into overall monitoring and control. In 1998 the Regulations for the Administration of Environmental Protection Concerning Construction Projects were issued, detailing the environment-impact-assessment (EIA) system, and the synchronized designing, construction and use of environmental-protection facilities together with the construction of relevant projects. The Environmental Impact Assessment Law, effective in 2003, expanded the EIA system from construction projects to all kinds of development plans, and stipulates that feasibility study meetings, hearings and other forms be introduced to discuss construction projects or plans with possible adverse impacts.

The main entities for environmental protection present a diversified structure with a widespread participation led by the government, promoted by enterprises, joined by the public, supported by science and technology, regulated by laws and adjusted by the market. NGOs and volunteers are playing significant roles in environmental protection.

Addressing Climate Change

China takes climate change very seriously in the course of its development. Bearing in mind the fundamental interests of the Chinese people and mankind's long-term development, it has exerted unremitting efforts to contribute to the fight against climate change.

On December 18, 2009 Premier Wen Jiabao delivered a speech titled, "Build Consensus and Strengthen Cooperation to Advance the Historical Process of Combating Climate Change" at the Copenhagen Climate Change Conference in Denmark. He said, "Climate change is a major global chal-

Electric cars passing the Tiananmen Rostrum

lenge. It is the common mission of the whole of mankind to curb global warming and save our planet. It is incumbent upon all of us, each and every country, nation, enterprise and individual to act, and act now in response to this challenge."

China was the first developing country to implement a National Climate Change Program. It has formulated or revised the Energy Conservation Law, Renewable Energy Law, Circular Economy Promotion Law, Clean Production Promotion Law, Forest Law, Grassland Law and Regulations on Civil Building Efficiency. Laws and regulations are an important means of addressing climate change.

China has made the most intensive efforts in energy conservation and emission reduction in recent years. It

Pushing for Concrete Results at Cancun

The climate change negotiations in Cancun, Mexico, held from November 29 to December 10, 2010, reached two final resolutions, facilitating the process of climate change negotiations. The draft bill presented to the conference by the Chinese delegation and the Group of 77 on the mitigation of climate change, which involves education, training and awareness issues, was unanimously adopted. It was the first point of consensus reached during the Cancun conference. China, India, Brazil and South Africa urged developed countries to accept the demand to submit detailed information on the financial, technical and capacity-building assistance they intend to transfer to developing countries.

has improved the taxation system and advanced the pricing reform of resource products with a view to putting in place at an early date a pricing mechanism that is responsive to market supply and demand, resource scarcity level and the costs of environmental damage. It has introduced major energy conservation projects and launched an energy conservation campaign, bringing energy-saving action to industry, transportation, construction and other key sectors. It has implemented pilot projects on the circular economy, promoted energy-saving and eco-friendly vehicles and subsidized households for using energy-saving products. It has worked hard to phase out backward production facilities that are energy-intensive and heavily polluting.

China has enjoyed the fastest growth in the world of new and renewable energy. On the basis of protecting the eco-environment, it has developed hydro power in an orderly way, and encouraged the exploitation of renewable energy, including solar and geothermal energy and wind power in the countryside, remote areas and other places with proper conditions. China has the largest area of man-made forests in the world. It is continuing its large-scale endeavors to return farmland to forest and expand forestation.

Geothermal heating system

Air Pollution Control

China began to control air pollution in the 1970s, mainly by preventing the emergence of new sources of pollution; and by strengthening the control and management of existing pollution sources.

In the early 1970s, it carried out a nationwide investigation on the quality of its air. In August 1973, it convened the First National Environmental Protection Meeting and in December promulgated the Trial Standards of Industrial "Three Wastes" Discharge, putting forward the "three-simultaneity" system that requires the prevention and control facilities targeting environmental pollution and other public hazards for new, rebuilding or expansion projects be designed, constructed and put into use simultaneously with the main projects.

In early 1996 China formulated a new Ambient Air Quality Standard, classifying floating dust as breathable particles, in an effort to further prevent air pollution.

In April 2004 an amended Law on the Prevention and Control of Atmospheric Pollution was adopted at the 15th meeting of the Ninth NPC Standing Committee. It was an important law in this regard and marked significant progress in China's efforts to prevent and control air pollution.

Historically speaking, China's air pollution control efforts have progressed from passively focusing on the treatment of sources to regional comprehensive prevention and control, and from using administrative management alone to resorting to legal and economic measures for protecting the environment.

Thanks to years of sustained pollution control, the air quality has seen great improvement. In 2009 the total volume of COD (chemical oxygen demand) emissions was 12.775 million tons, down by 3.27% over the previous year, and the total volume of SO_2 emissions was 22.144 million tons, a decrease of 4.60%.

Birds are flocking back as more forests are planted.

Water Pollution Control

China started its first large-scale pollution control project – the pollution investigation and control of the Guanting Reservoir – in 1972. The project lasted for eight years, and 112 pollution control programs were finished successively.

In August 1991 the Environmental Protection Commission under the State Council appointed the State Environmental Protection Administration (now Ministry of Environmental Protection) and the Ministry of Construction (now Ministry of Housing and Urban-Rural Development) to jointly hold the Second National Conference on Urban Environmental Protection. City governments at all levels were required to actively promote centralized pollution control, strengthen infrastructure, enhance protection of drinking water sources, improve urban rivers and lakes, and further conduct comprehensive improvement of the urban water environment. Those efforts slowed down the worsening of pollution in major cities, and some water environmental quality indices remained stable.

In February 1989 a pollution accident took place on the Huaihe River, threatening the life of millions of people and causing economic losses worth more than 100 million yuan. In 1993 the State Council decided to take the Huaihe River as a key environmental protection project, and carried out large-scale water basin treatment with the "three rivers" (Huaihe, Haihe and Liaohe) and the "three lakes" (Taihu, Chaohu and Dianchi) as the focus. This indicated that China's water pollution prevention and control had entered the phase of major river basin treatment.

Since 2003 the State Environmental Protection Administration has published annual updates on pollution control in key river basins and sea areas. Thanks to years of effort, there has been an obvious improvement in the water environment in the seriously polluted areas, and the Yellow River has not run dry for 11 consecutive years.

In 2007 the state spent several billion yuan on the Water Body Pollution Control and Treatment Program, focusing on drinking-water security, environmental control of river basins and urban water pollution treatment. The work on drinking-water security in the countryside will be strengthened, to solve this problem for 300 million rural people. The 12th Five-year Plan set such goals as to control the total discharge of major pollutants, adopt a strict protection system of drinking water sources, strengthen pollution treatment in such sectors as papermaking, printing and dying, chemical, leather manufacturing and large-scale livestock and poultry breeding, and continue water pollution prevention and control in major river basins and regions to guarantee drinking water safety for urban and rural residents.

Protection of Forest Resources

China's current forest coverage rate is 20.36%. Since the 1950s China has made amazing achievement in cultivating forests. Its total area of reserved planted forests ranks first in the world, and it carries out large-scale afforestation every year. While many countries have seen a decline in forest resources, China has seen increases in both area and reserves of its forests, and was listed by the United Nations Environmental Program as one of the 15 countries preserving the greatest area of forests. An effective program, started in 1998, put an end to the felling of trees in natural forests nationwide. In many areas, erstwhile lumbermen have now become forest rangers.

Nature Reserves

China's first nature reserve was the Dinghu Mountain Nature Reserve, established in 1956 in Zhaoqing, Guangdong Province. By the end of 2010, there had been about 2,590 nature reserves of various kinds, accounting for more than 15% of the country's land territory. Of them, about 320 are state-level ones. Protected through these nature reserves is about 90% of China's land eco-system, 90% of its wildlife population and nearly 70% of its higher plant communities.

Established in August 2000, the Sanjiangyuan Nature Reserve has the greatest concentration of bio-diversity of all of China's nature reserves. Covering an area of 31.6 million ha and with an average elevation of 4,000 m, it is also the largest and highest nature reserve in China. It is located in central Qinghai-Tibet Plateau, at the source of the Yangtze, Yellow and Lancang rivers. State funds totaling 220

Northern Tibet alpine prairie

Wetland Protection

China has 66 million ha of wetlands (including 39 million ha of natural wetlands), ranking first in Asia and fourth in the world. China's range of wetland types is among the widest in the world, with 31 types of natural wetlands and nine categories of artificial wetlands. Since joining the Ramsar Convention on Wetlands in 1992, China has established some 550 wetland nature reserves, and 37 have been classified as "Wetlands of International Significance."

Marine Protection

So far, more than 170 marine nature reserves of various kinds, including 32 national ones, have been established in China. They protect marine shoreline, estuary and island bio-environments, which possess great value for science and education; and also protect endangered marine animals such as the Indo-Pacific hump-backed dolphin (Sousa chinensis) and their habitats, as well as typical oceanic eco-systems such as mangroves, coral reefs and coastal wetlands.

The Law on Protection of the Ocean Environment covers the supervision and management of the ocean environment; surveying, monitoring, assessing and conducting of scientific research of the ocean environment; construction projects for control of ocean pollution; and ending ocean dumping pollution.

Sketch Map Showing Distribution of Major Nature Reserves and Wetlands

National Nature Reserves

Wetlands

Beijing ★

Harbin
Changchun
Shenyang
Hohhot
Tianjin
Yinchuan
Shijiazhuang
Xining
Taiyuan
Lanzhou
Jinan
Xi'an
Zhengzhou
Hefei
Chengdu
Nanjing
Shanghai
Wuhan
Hangzhou
Chongqing
Nanchang
Changsha
Guiyang
Fuzhou
Kunming
Taibei
Nanning
Guangzhou
Macao
Hong Kong
Haikou

Natural scenery of Jiuzhaigou   Swans at Rongcheng, Shandong Province

million yuan has been committed to the Sanjiangyuan protection project, which started in 2003.

Guangdong Province has about 300 nature reserves, the largest number in China. Wolong and Jiuzhaigou in Sichuan, Changbai Mountains in Jilin, Dinghu Mountains in Guangdong and Baishui River in Gansu and other nature reserves have been designated by the UNESCO as "World Biosphere Reserves."

Protecting Endangered Animals and Plants

China has rich biodiversity, boasting the world's largest number of bird species and gymnosperm varieties. But China's biodiversity is faced with a critical situation: 15% to 20% of its higher plant varieties are endangered, the numbers of 44% wild animals are declining, and the population of wild animals not under national protection is decreasing notably.

As one of the earliest signatory countries to the Convention on Biological Diversity, China has been active in international affairs concerning the Convention and vocal on important issues related to biodiversity. It is one of the few countries to have already completed the Convention's action plans.

The Convention demands every signatory country formulate or adjust its national strategies, plans or programs in accordance with its national conditions and in a timely fashion. The China Biological Diversity Protection Action Plan, finished in 1994, provides regulations for eco-environment protection activities. To date, the seven major targets stipulated in the Action Plan have been basically realized.

In recent years, with the emergence of such issues as genetically modified organisms, alien species invasion, and access to and benefit sharing of biological genetic resources, biological diversity protection is drawing increasing attention from the international community. The general trend of decline in biodiversity in China has not been checked, and the situation of biological species resources loss has not been fundamentally changed.

To implement the Convention, further strengthen its biodiversity protection, and effectively address new problems and meet new challenges arising in the course of biodiversity protection, China has compiled its Biodiversity Protection Strategy and Action Plan (2011-2030), putting forward overall goals, strategic tasks and priority actions for biodiversity protection in the coming 20 years.

So far, over 400 centers have been established for the raising of wild plant varieties or genetic protection, and artificial breeding of hundreds of wild plants. To help save endangered wildlife, 250 wildlife breeding centers have been established, and special projects have been conducted to protect seven species, including the giant panda and crested ibis. In accordance with the Law on the Protection of Wildlife, any criminal act damaging wildlife resources is subject to punishment.

ENGOs

There were 3,539 environmental non-governmental organizations (ENGOs) in China by October 2008. The All-China Environment Federation is the biggest and the most famous with certain government support. These organizations have organized various environmental campaigns such as "drive one day less," "26℃ limit for air-conditioners" and "protect the mother river."

Body painting themed on saving water resources

Twenty years have passed since Liu Detian, a press photographer in Panjin, Liaoning Province, founded China's first ENGO – the Black Beak Gull Protection Association – in 1991. Today the ENGOs have become a significant part of China's environmental-protection forces.

The period between 1991 and 2003 saw a cluster of ENGOs emerge. On June 5, 1993, World Environment Day, Liang Congjie and other 20 volunteers founded the Friends of Nature in Beijing. The Green Camp, founded by Tang Xiyang, recruited a large number of college students as "green" volunteers, many of whom later became avant-garde environmentalists. Touched by the story of Sonam Dargye, who sacrificed his life to protect Tibetan antelopes from poachers, Yang Xin has thrown himself into the protection of the source of the Yangtze River and the Tibetan antelopes. Other environmental activists include Liao Xiaoyi who founded the Global Village of Beijing, Wang Yongcheng, a journalist of China National Radio who founded the Green Earth Volunteers, Yang Yong, a folk scientist who led a group of volunteers to inspect glacial streams in southwest China, and Huo Daishan who founded the Huaihe River Guard with a group of volunteers.

As the Chinese society develops, acute problems such as regional environmental protection and increasing consumption-generated pollution keeps emerging, and individual environmentalists get involved into various social conflicts, especially environmental ones.

In this regard there has been a long-standing argument over the abuse of hydropower in southwest China, when the ENGOs start to exercise their supervision over social management. They have pursued environmental assessment of major

Making
recyclable bags

economic activities, such as the real estate development on Purple Mountain in Nanjing, Jiangxi Province.

The ENGOs also combine their efforts for greater influence. The Green Choice Alliance Program was born from this.

The Green Choice Alliance Program was initiated by 21 ENGOs in 2007, including the Institution of Public & Environmental Affairs led by Ma Jun, the Friends of Nature, the Green Earth Volunteers and the Global Village of Beijing. The Green Choice Alliance Program calls on the public not to buy products made by polluting enterprises, thus prevent their products from

Liao Xiaoyi

entering the market. As the program expands, it has attracted social attention by intensifying supervision over polluting enterprises. Inspired by them, some influential media, including China Central Television, have exposed and questioned the conduct of polluting enterprises.

The "26℃ limit for air-conditioners" activity initiated by Liao Xiaoyi, Wang Yongchen and others in Beijing was finally adopted by the Chinese government as a state policy.

In recent years the ENGOs have been constantly making their voices heard on major international and domestic environmental issues. They have also participated in the decision making for major economic activities involving the ecological environment.

International Cooperation

China actively supports global environmental efforts, and plays a constructive role in international environmental affairs. To date, it has acceded to over 50 international conventions concerning environmental protection, and actively performs its obligations. The Chinese government has promulgated more than 100 policies and measures on the protection of the ozonosphere and met the gradual reduction goals stipulated in the Montreal Protocol on Substances That Deplete the Ozone Layer.

The China Council for Cooperation on Environment and Development was created by China as the first body of its kind in the world. It consists of some 40 experts and serves as a senior consultancy for the government. It has made many constructive proposals to the Chinese government, and is regarded overseas as a model of international environmental cooperation.

China actively participates in and promotes regional cooperation on environmental protection, having formed an initial cooperation framework with others, including the China-Japan-Korea Tripartite Environment Ministers Meeting, the China-Europe mechanism for the ministerial dialogue on environmental policies, the Asia-Europe Ministers Meeting, the environmental cooperation with Arabic states and the environmental cooperation mechanisms under the framework of the Shanghai Cooperation Organization.

China maintains good cooperative relations with the United Nations Environment Program, the United Nations Development Program, the Global Environment Facility, the World Bank and the Asian Development Bank. Bilateral cooperation agreements and memorandums have been signed between China and the US, Japan and Russia. A number of cooperative projects have been implemented under bilateral gratis programs with the European Union, Germany and Canada or international organizations.

The global ENGOs, among them the Worldwide Fund for Nature and the International Fund for Animal Welfare, cooperate with Chinese authorities and ENGOs, with positive results.

Southern slope of Mount Qomolangma

At a precision equipment company

Education and Science

Through unremitting efforts over the past 60 years, especially the past 30 years of reform and opening up, China, a developing country with a population of 1.3 billion, has established the largest education system in the world, including nine-year compulsory gratis education, fast-growing vocational education, and mass higher education with increasingly higher standards. Educational development will accelerate China's transformation from merely being a populous country to a major human resources power.

Education System

China has implemented nine-year compulsory gratis education. Preschool education includes kindergartens and other forms; after compulsory education, education includes standard high schools, secondary specialized schools; and higher education includes junior college and above. All types of continuing education also exist.

Higher Education	Postgraduate
	University and College
	Polytechnic and Vocational College
Secondary Education	Secondary Vocational School
	Secondary Technical School
	High School (Junior and Senior)
Primary Education	Primary School
	Kindergarten and Preschool
Adult Education, Military College, Private College, Religious College	
Special Education	
Continuing Education, On-job Education	

China has the world's largest number of people receiving formal education. Over 300 million people are in schools of various kinds. Net elementary school enrollment has reached 99.5%; and gross enrollment rates in junior and senior high schools, and higher-learning institutions are, respectively, 98%, 66% and 26.5%. Nine-year compulsory education is in effect in over 95% of China's populated areas, with illiteracy in the young and middle-aged population under 4%. Education in China has reached the average level of middle-income countries.

Foreign pupils are a common sight in China's metropolises.

Concentrating in class

Secondary vocational school students dismantling automobile engines

Nine-year compulsory gratis education is the foundation of China's education system. As a populous country, China attaches great importance to basic education. The funds for the nine-year compulsory education have been fully incorporated into the national financial system. This is a historic change in China's education system, realizing the centuries-old ideal that "in education, there should be no distinction of social status."

Having ensured schooling for almost all children, the government is turning to deal with unbalanced allocation of compulsory educational resources: give preferential treatment to rural, ethnic-minority, border and poverty-stricken areas in allocation of educational resources nationwide or within a province (region or city); and give preferential treatment to disadvantaged schools within a city or county to achieve a balanced allocation of teachers, equipment, books and school buildings. Due to disparities in local economic and social development, the problem of unbalanced development of compulsory education won't be solved in a short period of time.

For non-compulsory education, the government has initiated effective ways of assistance, mainly including scholarships and stipends, to safeguard the basic right of every citizen to receive further education. The Central Government allocation to provide scholarships and stipends for ordinary undergraduate students and students in higher and secondary vocational schools increased from 2.05 billion yuan in 2006 to 26 billion yuan in 2010. In the coming years, more money will be allocated to raise the amount of scholarships and stipends, expand their coverage, and provide guarantees and discounts for student loans in line with the characteristics of all forms of education. The funds aim to cover tuition fees and basic living expenses for students with economic difficulties. Correspondingly, a certain proportion of tuition fees is used to aid poor students. The government encourages all sectors of society to offer scholarships and stipends in various forms, and encourage students to join work-study programs to help pay for their own education.

The schooling of children from special groups. Rapid industrialization and urbanization in China have brought about large numbers of rural migrant workers. This had made the schooling of their children a big problem. The government is endeavoring to ensure they receive free education at full-time state schools. Chinese laws and regulations have defined the right to education of people with disabilities: in addition to schools for special education, disabled children capable of adapting to regular study conditions can enroll in standard elementary and high schools. The government will speed up the building of schools for special education, and create conditions for more students with disabilities to attend standard schools.

As more than half of the total population and school-age children are living in the countryside, rural education is especially important in China. Over the years, rural education has been progressing smoothly. Since 2007 the state has exempted rural students from tuition fees during the compulsory education period, and provided them with free textbooks. This has significantly reduced the amount of illiteracy there. In addition, efforts have been intensified to promote the training of rural teachers. In 2007 the State Council approved a pilot project to provide free education to would-be teachers in the universities directly under the administration of the Ministry

Demonstrating a multi-functional lift robot at the National University Students' Machinery Innovative Design Competition

Project Hope

"Project Hope" is a public welfare program carried out by the China Youth Development Foundation since 1989. It aims at financing dropped-out students in poverty-stricken areas to return to school, establishing schools and improving rural educational conditions. Donations to establish Project Hope schools and financing poor students are the two major programs of Project Hope.

On May 20, 2007 Project Hope shifted from its "rescue one child" mode toward "rescue plus development," paying more attention to impoverished students' potential for self-improvement. More financial programs, e.g., work-study and social practice, are added for all assisted students on the basis of existing stipends.

of Education, contributing to the training of rural teachers. However, with unbalanced development among different regions, China is still facing educational problems in some underdeveloped rural areas, including sparsely furnished schools.

China's educational horizons are expanding, with the number of candidates for master's degrees and higher continuing to soar. The education market has skyrocketed; and training and examination for professional qualifications such as computer science and foreign languages are booming. Continuing education is the trend.

Investment in education has increased, with the money from the overall budget allocated to education being raised by over one percentage point annually since 1998. Following a Ministry of Education program, the government will set up an educational financing system that matches the public finance system, emphasizing the responsibilities of governments at all levels for funding education, and ensuring faster growth of their financial allocations for education than that of regular revenues. The program also expects government education expenditure to expand to 4% of the GDP in a short period of time.

The first Law on the Promotion of Private Education came into effect on September 1, 2003. The development of private schools means an increase in overall education supply and a change in the traditional pattern of government-funded schools only to meet public education needs.

Education Planning

The Outline of the National Program for Long- and Medium-term Education Reform and Development (2010-2020) was China's first educational plan in the 21st century. It provides guidelines for China's education reform and development. At the present stage, institutional reform is the key to education reform. The Outline focuses on major issues, including institutional and teaching reforms in elementary, vocational and higher-learning institutions, and teacher training, which will have a great impact on China's reform of its educational system.

Tsinghua University

According to the Outline, by 2020 China will basically realize education modernization, and become a human resources power. The Outline sets higher targets for education popularization: to make preschool education basically universal; improve the quality of nine-year compulsory education; popularize high school education, with a gross enrolment rate of 90%; accelerate the popularization of higher education, with a gross enrolment rate of 40%; eliminate illiteracy in the young and middle-aged population; extend the average schooling duration of incoming labor force from today's 12.4 years to 13.5 years; extend the average schooling duration of the working-age population from today's 9.5 years to 11.2 years, and give 20% of them higher education, doubling the figure for 2009.

A campus in autumn

The Outline also emphasizes equal access to education for all. China will establish a basic public education system covering both urban and rural areas, achieve the equalization of basic public education step by step, and narrow the gaps among regions; effectively promote equal access to compulsory education of children of migrant workers; and safeguard the right to education of people with disabilities.

To meet the skyrocketing demand for highly skilled workers, the state is working on two vocational education programs: training personnel urgently needed for the modern manufacturing and service industries, and training rural labor migrating to urban areas.

Practicing Chinese calligraphy

International Exchanges

China is seeing active cooperation and exchanges in education with the rest of the world. Exchange students are a major part of this, and no other country has more people studying abroad than China. Meanwhile, the number of foreign students has also increased rapidly. Since New China was founded in 1949, especially over the

World Culture Festival held at Beijing's Foreign Languages and Cultures University

past 30 years of reform and opening up, China has received 1.69 million students from over 190 countries and regions, including 240,000 currently studying in the country. Overseas students have become an important bridge for promoting friendly exchanges between Chinese people and the people of other countries. The Chinese government will offer more scholarships to attract foreign students.

The introduction of high-quality educational resources is also a trend. China plans to absorb more world-class experts and scholars to teach, do scientific research and handle management in China, and bring in top overseas professionals and academic groups in a planned way; introduce excellent teaching materials from abroad; increase the proportion of foreign teachers in institutions of higher learning; and attract Chinese citizens studying abroad to return after finishing their studies.

Today, learning the Chinese language has become a popular pursuit around the world. Since 2004 China has opened not-for-profit Confucius Institutes overseas, with the aim of spreading the Chinese language and culture. By October 2010, 691 Confucius Institutes and schools had been established in 96 countries and regions.

Science and Technology

A hundred years ago, China had no modern science and technology at all – fewer than 10 people in the country understood calculus. But by the early 21st century the hi-tech research and development gap between China and the advanced countries had shrunk visibly; 60% of China's technology sector, including atomic energy, space technology, high-energy physics, biosciences, computer and information technology and robotics, have reached or are close to the advanced world levels. The successful launches of manned spacecraft in 2003 and 2005, as well as the launch of a moon probe satellite in 2007, marked a leap in Chinese astronautics. In September 2008 China launched the manned Shenzhou VII, and a Chinese astronaut made China's first-ever space walk. China became the world's third country to master the technologies required for space walks. On October 24, 2007 the first Chinese-made lunar probe – Chang'e-1 – was launched, which brought back

Chang'e-2 lifting off into space

the first 3D map of the entire lunar surface; Chang'e-2 was successfully launched on October 1, 2010. According to the Lunar Exploration Program, China will finish gathering moon soil samples before 2020.

The Law on the Progress of Science and Technology, promulgated in 1993, provides basic guidance for China's scientific and technological development. It clarifies the goal and role of development, funding sources and awards regarding scientific and technological achievements. The Law on the Popularization of Science and Technology, promulgated in 2002, makes it a societal goal to popularize science and technology among all citizens. Local regulations have been issued for attracting talented people, ensuring investment in science and technology, and developing high technology.

In February 2006 the State Council issued its Guidelines for the National Medium- and Long-term Program for Science and Technology Development (2006-2020). This outlines a plan to speed up research in 16 major or key technologies in the next 15 years, covering strategic industries such as information and biosciences; important and urgent issues concerning energy, resources, environment and health; and also R&D for large aircraft, manned space flight and the Moon Probe Project. By 2020 China's overall investment in research and experimentation is expected to top 2.5% of its GDP, compared with 1.33% in 2005; and the progress of science and technology will contribute over 60% to China's development.

Innovations in Science and Technology

Investment in science and technology has been greatly increased over the 60 years since New China was founded. In 1953 a total of 56 million yuan was allocated for science and technology. In the 21st century China is enhancing the capability of independent innovation as the basic strategy of its science and technology development. Governments at all levels provide strong financial support for independent innovations. In 2008 the state allocated over 240 billion yuan for science and technology, up by more than 40 times compared with the figure for 1978. In 2009, though the state tightened its monetary policy to deal with the international financial crisis, the central government invested 146.1 billion yuan in science and technology, an increase of 25.6% over the previous year. The spending on science by local governments also see notable increases.

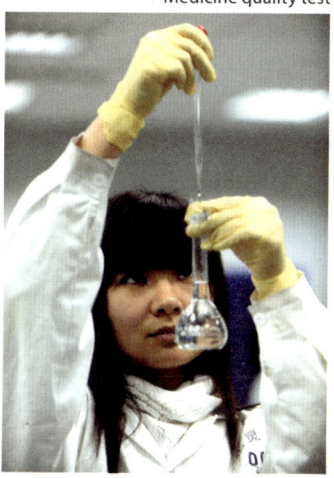

Medicine quality test

Many of China's agricultural science and technology achievements are leading the world, among them bird-flu vaccine, insect-resistant cotton, dwarf-male-sterile wheat, super-

Power-generation models at a science and technology exposition

CAS and CAE

The Chinese Academy of Sciences (CAS) is China's highest academic institute and comprehensive research center for natural sciences. Its academic divisions are those of mathematics and physics, chemistry, geography, and technological sciences. Moreover, it has 12 branch academies, 100 subordinate research institutes, and more than 100 national key laboratories and engineering centers across the country.

The Chinese Academy of Engineering (CAE) is the country's highest honorary consultative institute in engineering science and technology, conducting strategic studies of the state's important engineering-related issues and providing consultation for decision-making.

The title of CAS or CAE academician is the highest academic one in science and technology. Both also have foreign academicians.

high-yield rice, and low-erucic-acid and low-glucosinolate oilseed. China has also developed and applied a wealth of key generic technologies in the fields of precision manufacturing, clean energy, intelligent transportation and information security; and made breakthroughs in core technologies significant for urban environmental pollution control, resource exploration and utilization, natural-disaster alleviation and prevention, and ecological protection. It has also achieved many innovative successes in frontier fields such as micro-electronic and photo-electronic materials, functional ceramics, nano-materials, and biomedical materials.

National key bases have been established for innovations in science and technology. For instance, the SSRF (Shanghai Synchrotron Radiation Facility) and I-Most set up during the 11th Five-year Plan period (2006-2010) have laid a solid foundation for future development in this field. China's supercomputer Tianhe-1 with domestically developed CPUs has been put into use at the National Center for Supercomputing in Tianjin. The new technical data of Tianhe-1 has showed its superb performance in calculation.

International Cooperation

China has developed sci-tech cooperation with over 150 countries and regions, signing cooperation agreements with about 100 of them, and has joined more than 1,000 international sci-tech cooperation organizations. Non-governmental, international sci-tech cooperation and exchanges have become more active in recent years, ranging from staff exchanges to joint

R&D to make breakthroughs in core technologies.

More than 200 Chinese scientists hold leading positions at all levels in important international organizations. China plays an active role in cooperation concerning major international scientific projects, covering the fields of nuclear fusion, reactors, Intel CPU, human genome, and IODP (Integrated Ocean Drilling Program).

The International Scientific and Technological Cooperation Award is a national prize established by the State Council to be granted to foreign scientists, engineers, managers or organizations for their contributions to bilateral or multilateral sci-tech cooperation. More than one foreign expert wins the honor annually.

An ocean exploration expedition preparing for an experiment

Social Sciences

China has more than 100,000 researchers engaged in social sciences. The Chinese Academy of Social Sciences (CASS), established in 1977, is the top academic organization in this field, by virtue of its comprehensive scope and concentration of professional skills, data and research materials. It is known for creative theoretical exploration and policy research. The Academy has 31 institutes and 45 research centers, with over 3,200 researchers. In addition, 1,676 of the staff are senior experts, including many well known in international academic circles, or younger and middle-age researchers distinguished for theoretical studies.

In August 2006, the CASS established five academic divisions: literature, history and philosophy; economics; social politics and law; international research; and Marxism. More academic divisions are planned. The academic status of CASS members is equivalent to that of CAS academicians.

Life and Culture

China is the world's largest developing country, with a population of more than 1.3 billion. By the poverty standards defined by the World Bank, the Chinese government has lifted over 0.5 billion people out of poverty in 20 years. Great changes have taken place in the Chinese people's life, compared to what it was in the early period of the founding of New China over 60 years ago.

Suburban touring

Social Life

Income and Consumption

A major goal of the 12th Five-year Plan (2011-2015) is a 7% annual increase of the GDP, with per-capita disposable income of urban residents and per-capita net income of rural residents both rising above 7%. The Plan explicitly stipulates that the income increase should be higher than that of the GDP.

The per-capita net income of rural residents in 2010 was 5,919 yuan, up 10.9% year-on-year, and the per-capita disposable income of urban residents was 19,109 yuan, up 7.8%. With the improvement of the living conditions of both rural and urban residents, China's consumption structure has been transformed to one allowing extra consumption from simply covering the basic need for food and clothing. Today, the Chinese are spending on education, housing, automobiles, computers, stocks and overseas travel. Living conditions have likewise further improved. Clothing, food, housing and transportation are all showing great changes, reflecting greater interest in fashion, nutrition and home comfort. Traveling by taxi or in one's own car has become commonplace.

New domains in which the consumption is expanding the fastest include private cars, telecommunication, housing, education and travel.

According to the National Bureau of Statistics, the number of private cars shows an annual increase rate of above 20%. Some major cities, like Beijing, have begun to adopt policies to restrict car purchases in order to avoid or reduce traffic jams, and reduce emissions while accelerating the development of public transportation.

As the housing problem concerns the national economy and people's livelihood, the government has since 2003 begun to control the real estate market. Since late 2009 the State Council has adopted a series of measures, including regulating the market order, improving policies on land, revenue, taxation and finance, curbing the speculation, directing the market to supply more ordinary commercial housing, accelerating construction of low-income housing, developing public rental housing and promoting a rational housing supply structure.

As for travel consumption, tourism has boomed along with the increase of disposable income and free time of both rural and urban residents. In coming years the per-capita consumption level will keep rising and service consumption will be as high as merchandise consumption. As free time, like holidays and weekends, is catching up with that of the moderately developed countries, a huge tourism consumption market will take shape, and tourism will be an important part of the life of urban residents. By 2015, tourism consumption will account for 10% of the total consumption of urban residents.

By the end of 2010 China's total population had reached 1.339 billion, among whom urban residents numbered 630 million. So far, the per-capita consumption expense of rural residents, who are the majority of China's population, only accounts for one third of that of urban residents. Therefore, rural consumption has become the focus of efforts to expand domestic demand. The consumption in rural areas is still oriented toward basic living needs and agricultural materials,

Bicycling

with a low degree of purchase of computers and cars. China has resorted to special revenues and trade policies for years to produce reliable and less-costly electrical appliances, cars and motorcycles in rural areas to stimulate the consumption market there.

Employment

Research reports predict that the total population on China's mainland will surpass 1.52 billion by 2050. That is to say that in the coming 40 years new urban labor forces and unemployed and surplus rural labor forces will increase every year. China is responding to an unprecedented challenge – with only 9.4% of the world's natural resources, 9.4% of its capital resources and 1.85% of its intellectual and technical resources, it has to provide jobs for a labor force accounting for 26% of the world's population.

The 12th Five-year Plan puts forward the strategy of putting employment first, and encourages industries and production services helpful for increasing employment and developing human resources. This means the government will take more active employment policies, expand the scale of employment and self-employment, and work hard to solve the employment problems of college graduates, migrant workers and the poor in urban areas. These measures include enlarging vocational training for migrant workers and providing more supportive policies for self-employment. In the coming five years, nine million new urban jobs will be created each year, and the registered unemployment rate will be confined within 5%.

Migrant workers going out in urban construction

Social Security

The government vows to basically establish a social security system that covers all rural and urban residents by 2020, which will comprise various types of social insurance, subsistence allowance and aid, charities and commercial insurance. All these are expected to provide the largest social security system in the world.

China's social security system came into being from scratch after the founding of New China in 1949. After years of effort, a framework of social security with Chinese characteristics has been primarily established. It's no comparison to those of the developed countries and is only able to guarantee the basic living of its citizens in five aspects: basic old-age insurance, basic medical insurance, unemployment insurance, work injury insurance and maternity insurance. The old-age insurance maintains a moderate living standard for workers after retirement; the unemployment insurance maintains subsistence for workers in case of unemployment; and the medical insurance covers ordinary medical needs for the insured.

Besides the above "five insurances," there is also the Housing Provident Fund. The insurance fees for old-age, medical and unemployment insurances are shared by enterprises and individuals, while those for work injury and maternity insurances are all paid by the employers.

The payment quota for the "five insurances and one fund" varies in different areas, with the total salary as the base amount. Taking Beijing for instance, the payment proportion for old-age insurance by enterprises and individuals is 20% and 8%, respectively; for medical insurance, 10% and 2% plus three yuan; and for unemployment insurance, 1.5% and 0.5%. The payment, accounting for 0.5% to 2% of the employee's salary, for work injury insurance is shouldered by enterprises. The payment, accounting for 0.8% of the employee's salary, for maternity insurance is also paid by enterprises. The Beijing government stipulates that enterprises and employees should undertake the same payment, which accounts for 12% of the employees' salaries, for the Housing Provident Fund. This is helpful for medium- and low-income employees to solve their housing problems.

Since 1990 the State Council has promulgated the Regulations on Unemployment Insurance, Interim Regulations on the Collection of Social Insurance Premiums, and Regulations on Subsistence Allowances to Urban Residents, providing legal guarantees for the implementation of the social security system.

From only state- and collective-owned enterprises, social insurance coverage has expanded to non-public enterprises and institutions, as well as to those who are flexibly employed.

A subsistence allowance system has been established in all cities and county towns, providing basic guarantees for residents with family income below the minimum local standard. The productivity still remains at a low level in some places, and differs a lot in different regions. With the development of China's economy and society, the level of subsistence allowance will increase continuously as the revenues at all levels keep increasing.

Rural Social Old-age Insurance

China's rural social old-age insurance integrates individual payment with collective subsidies and government allowances.

The insurance account comprises of base pension and individual pension account. The base pension is guaranteed by the national revenue, meaning rural residents at the age of 60 and above will enjoy a national universally-beneficial old-age pension. This insurance will cover all farmers before 2020.

In 2002 China launched a new rural cooperative medical care system. Focused on major-illness health insurance coverage, the system is based on payment by individuals, financial support from the collective, and subsidies from the government. If a farmer who has joined the scheme is hospitalized, some incurred costs can be reimbursed according to a sliding scale. Although this system remains at a low level in terms of fund collection, it will cover the most people in the world – over 800 million. The funds are only spent on medical expenses incurred by rural dwellers, and are forbidden to be used for other purpose. Besides, an open and transparent supervision system has also been established.

A standard rural medical-aid system has been established throughout the country, offering free medical treatment to poor farmers who are seriously ill. The funds, raised from special allocations at various levels of government and from voluntary donations from society, are used exclusively for free medical services.

During the period of the 12th Five-year Plan, China's total population will be controlled within 1.39 billion. The Plan envisages the average lifespan increasing by 1.5 years to 74.5 years; the new rural cooperative medical care system achieving nationwide coverage; the number of urban dwellers covered by basic old-age insurance reaching 375 million; the insurance coverage rate of the three basic medical care insurance schemes in urban and rural areas increasing by three percentage points; 36 million new low-income urban apartments being built; and the size of the poverty-stricken population continuing to shrink.

Medical Care and Health

For every 1,000 people, China has 1.75 doctors and 3.31 hospital beds. In Beijing, Shanghai, Tianjin, Chongqing and other large cities, general hospitals and hospitals specializing in such areas as cancer, cardio- and cerebro-vascular disorders, ophthalmology, dentistry and infectious diseases can be found. Medium-sized cities have general and specialized hospitals with modern facilities. Medical treatment, disease prevention, and healthcare networks have taken shape at county, township and village levels. Central and district hospitals, and clinics have been set up in counties, towns and administrative villages, respectively.

With the establishment of health and medical care organizations, along with the steady spread of better hygiene habits, infectious and parasitic diseases that were formerly major killers have been replaced by cancer, cardio- and cerebro-vascular diseases, creating a mortality pattern closer to that of developed countries. The health of urban and rural residents has thus been greatly improved, and the average life expectancy is now 73.0 years, close to the levels of the moderately developed countries.

"Prevention first" is one of the important principles in the health care work. All administrative levels have established hygiene and disease-prevention organizations responsible for the overall management of these functions, including hygiene and epidemic-prevention stations, forming a nationwide network of hygiene super-

Physical examination for blood donation

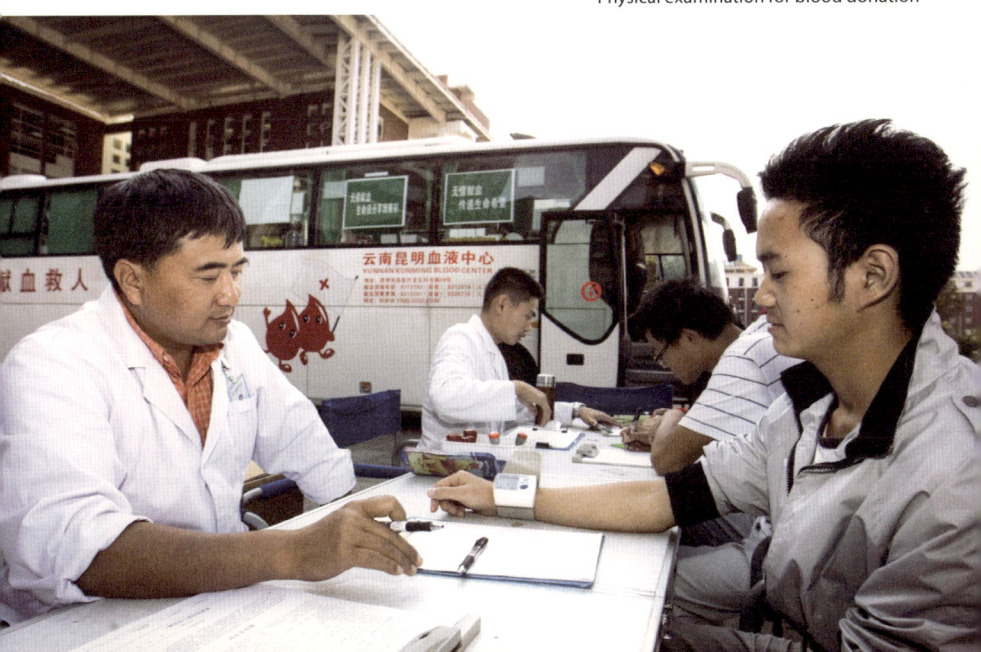

vision and control. In May 2003 the State Council issued its Regulations on Public Health Emergency Responses, establishing a legal framework for tackling public-health crises.

Since the reform of the medical and public health systems deepened in 2009, the number of urbanites covered by medical care insurance has increased by 114 million. The three basic medical care systems – new rural cooperative medical care, urban workers medical insurance and non-working urban resident medical insurance – now cover over 1.26 billion people. The goal of covering all Chinese citizens with medical care insurance is being nearly realized.

During the 12th Five-year Plan period, the reform of the medical and health care systems will be continued to guarantee all Chinese people basic medical care as quickly as possible. Basic old-age insurance and medical care security will attain full coverage, and the coverage rate of the three basic medical care insurance schemes will be increased steadily. In addition, medical care insurance reimbursement will surpass 70%.

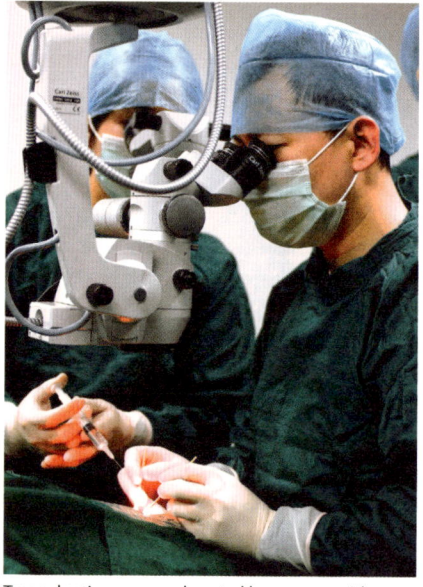
Transplanting cornea donated by a young girl

Traditional Chinese Medicine

Compared with Western medicine, traditional Chinese medicine (TCM) has its independent theoretical and diagnostic methods, such as observation, pulse-taking and acupuncture, with herbal medicine as its main form of treatment. Its unique medical effects have long been acknowledged through clinical practice. Most general hospitals in China have set up TCM departments.

TCM and Western Medicine

The medical treatment with medication commonly applied worldwide, referred to by the Chinese as "Western medicine," is available across the country through relatively high-level clinical treatment. Both traditional Chinese and Western medical treatments are being used by China's medical professionals, particularly to diagnose and cure difficult and complicated cases. There are 236 hospitals providing such combined treatments, with a staff of over 70,000. Combined medical treatments are also offered by most general hospitals.

Sports and Physical Fitness

Mass Sports

China has more than one million sports venues of all kinds, 240 times the number in the early period of New China. A survey released by the General Administration of Sports indicates that more than 60% of urban residents use sports clubs for physical fitness activities, and over 95% of students have attained the National Physical Exercise Standard.

Nationwide Body-building Program

The Physical Health Law was adopted in 1995. In the same year the State Council promulgated its Outline of a Nationwide Body-building Program.

Aiming to improve the health and physical condition of the general public, the Nationwide Body-building Program encourages everyone, youth and children in particular, to engage in at least one sports activity a day, learn at least two ways of keeping fit, and have a health examination every year.

Through this 15-year-long program, the government aims to build a sports and fitness service system for the general public. Most gymnasiums and

National Body-building Day

To meet the increasing need for sports by the Chinese people and encourage more to join in physical fitness activities, every August 8 has been set aside as National Body-building Day since 2009. Departments in charge of sports activities at county level and above will provide free body-building guidance on this day, and all public sports facilities will open to the public free.

Skating

stadiums across China are open to the general public. Outdoor fitness centers have been installed in urban communities, public parks, squares, roadsides and other convenient locations, equipped with various forms of exercise facilities.

By 2015, body-building will become a basic way of life for more people, and over 90% of the population (students excluded) is expected to attain the National Physique Evaluation Standard.

Sports Meets

China has five large-scale sports competitions held once every four years: National Games, National Farmers' Games, National University Games, National Games for the Disabled, and National Minorities Traditional Sports Games. The National Games are comprehensive athletic games at the highest level, held 11 times so far since 1959. The 12th National Games will be held in September 2013. The National Farmers' Games have been held since 1988. The National University Games have been held since 1982. The

Hurdling

National Games for the Disabled have been held since 1984. In November 1953 the first National Minorities Traditional Sports Games was held, aimed at preserving these traditional sports and setting competitive standards for them.

Traditional Sports

Traditional sports with distinct Chinese characteristics are very popular, including *wushu* (martial arts), *taijiquan* (Chinese shadow-boxing), *qigong*, *xiangqi* (Chinese chess) and *weiqi* (go).

Wushu combines exercise with arts of self-defense, including bare-fisted box-ing as well as the use of offensive and defensive apparatus, with different schools

Taijiquan

Yak racing on the Qinghai-Tibet Plateau

and moves. *Taijiquan* emphasizes bodily movement following mind movement, and tempering robustness with gentleness and graceful postures. Mainly a system of deep breathing exercises, *qigong* is a unique Chinese way of keeping fit, aimed at enhancing health, prolonging life, treating illness and improving physiological functions, by focusing the mind and regulating the breathing.

The variety of entertaining and competitive sports activities in minority areas includes wrestling and horsemanship of the Mongol, Uyghur and Kazak people; Tibetan yak racing; Korean "seesaw jumping" and swinging; Miao crossbow; and the dragon-boat races of the Dai.

Competitive Sports

On June 7, 1956 China's weightlifter Chen Jingkai broke the world record for the clean and jerk in a Sino-Soviet friendly competition, becoming China's first athlete to set a world record. In 1959 China's table-tennis player Rong Guotuan won the gold medal at the 25th World Table Tennis Championships, becoming the first world champion in New China's sporting history. China's pistol shooter Xu Haifeng got China's first Olympic gold medal in the 1984 Summer Olympics in Los Angeles, helping the Chinese delegation reach the fourth place in the gold medal tally, with 15 gold medals. At the 2008 Summer Olympics in Beijing, China won the most gold medals, and was in second place in the total of medals. China first participated in the Winter Olympics in 1980, and short-track speed skater Yang Yang reaped China's first gold medal at the Salt Lake City Winter Olympics in 2002.

Li Na reaped champion of women's single at the 2011 French Open.

Ping-pong is one of China's major competitive sports

In this century, young Chinese athletes have begun to demonstrate increasing maturity on the world stage. Hurdler Liu Xiang, basketball players Yao Ming and Yi Jianlian, rowers Meng Guanliang and Yang Wenjun, tennis players Li Na, Sun Tiantian, Li Ting, Yan Zi and Zheng Jie, and snooker player Ding Junhui are all examples of top-class athletes.

The credit for China's achievements in competitive sports should go to its training system. It has its base in the juvenile amateur sports schools and basic-level clubs, with teams representing localities as the backbone, and the national team at the highest level. The training system ensures that China's elite teams maintain a year-round squad of about 20,000 outstanding athletes. On February 3, 2004 the State Council proclaimed its Anti-Doping Regulations, the country's first detailed stipulations concerning the control of performance-enhancing drugs, anti-doping obligations, examination and monitoring, and legal liabilities. The Regulations came into force March 1, 2004.

Sports for People with Disabilities

Chinese sports for the disabled play a leading role in the world, and have made many excellent achievements in world-class competitions. In terms of gold metals, the Chinese team entered top 10 at the Atlanta Paralympics in 1996, and led in the number of medals at the Athens Paralympics in 2004 and the Beijing Paralympics in 2008.

The establishment of the National Paralympics Committee in 1983 institution-alized the sports for people with disabilities. The China Sports Association for the Deaf and Special Olympics China were established in 1985 and 1986, respectively; and sports associations for people with disabilities in each province, autonomous region and municipality have also been set up. China has already joined eight comprehensive international sports organizations for people with disabilities, as well as international organizations for particular sports. Shanghai hosted the 2007 Special Olympics International, while Beijing hosted the 2008 Paralympics Games.

Culture and Arts

National Library of China

In recent years, reform of the cultural system has been car-ried out widely, featuring en-hanced public cultural services and abundant cultural prod-ucts. Over the past five years, the task of transforming public institutions into enterprises has basically been completed in the spheres of publishing, circulation and movie and TV program production. To build a unified, open, competitive and orderly market system, China will accel-erate reform and innovation of the cultural sphere, promote the corporatization of for-profit cultural institutions and steadily carry out reform of non-profit ones.

Libraries

China has nearly 3,000 public libraries with a total of over 550 million volumes and copies. Public libraries have been set up across the country. Among university libraries, the libraries of Peking and Wuhan universities have the biggest collec-tions. The national library network also comprises libraries of scientific research

View inside the National Library of China

institutions, various primary-level entities, and elementary and high schools.

With a collection of 27 million volumes and copies, and digital resources of 250 terabits, the National Library of China is the largest library in Asia. It boasts 730,000 precious documents, of which, the amount and quality of its ancient tortoiseshells carved with Chinese pictographs, documents from the Dunhuang Grottoes, records of different places and scripts of celebrities lead both domestic and overseas libraries. As a general book storehouse of China, it has collected most of the books, magazines and newspapers published in contemporary China. It also has the most foreign documents with a collection of 10.776 million volumes. The library began to accept submissions of official publications in 1916, and domestic electronic publications in 1987. It is China's ISSN (International Standard Serial Number) Center and Network Information Center.

The library has formed a digital library alliance with others across the country to promote China's digital public information service. It has set up 13 databases covering electronic books, newspaper resources, rare books and reference works. The Digital Library makes the National Library the world's largest Chinese literature collection center and digital resource base, as well as the most advanced information network service base in China.

Shanghai Library is China's largest provincial-level library. It has a collection of over 1.7 million volumes of ancient documents, among which there are 25,000 titles of rare books in 178,000 volumes, many being the only surviving copies anywhere. The earliest document dates back about 1,500 years.

By the end of 2011 all public libraries and cultural centers will realize free admission for all, open all public areas and facilities for free and provide free basic services.

Museums

There are more than 2,400 government-sponsored and non-governmental museums in China. With a total collection surpassing 20 million items, these museums hold nearly 10,000 exhibitions a year. Museums based on cultural relics, like the Museum of the Qin Terracotta Warriors and Horses in Xi'an, attract countless visitors from both at home and abroad. The government encourages exchanges of cultural relics between museums, as well as displays and exchanges of legitimate private collections. By 2015 China will build another 1,000 museums, so that every city of medium size or larger will possess at least one.

The Palace Museum has a rich collection of cultural relics.

On the east of Tiananmen Square in Beijing, the National Museum of China integrates a variety of functions – archeological findings, collection, research and display, and possesses more than one million items of ancient, modern and contemporary Chinese relics as well as over one million of literary documents. Its total area of 200,000 sq m makes the museum the world's largest.

China's First Private Museum

The Guanfu Museum, established in 1996 by Ma Weidu, a leading Beijing collector of cultural relics, was China's first private museum. It was nominated one of China's top 10 private museums in 2004. The museum displays traditional Chinese porcelain works, furniture, oil paintings, craftworks, and windows and doors, in addition to a video hall and a multifunctional hall.

Preservation of Cultural Relics

World-famous archeological sites in China include the Peking Man site at Zhoukoudian near Beijing, Mausoleum of the First Emperor of the Qin Dynasty (221-206 BC), Mawangdui Han Dynasty (202 BC-220 AD) Tomb in Changsha, Dunhuang Grottoes in Gansu Province and the underground palace of the Famen Temple in Shaanxi Province.

However, many of China's most precious cultural and historical relics were removed during the troubles of the 19th and 20th centuries. The UNESCO estimates that 1.64 million Chinese cultural relics are in the collections of more than 200 museums in 47 countries, and the number of Chinese cultural relics collected by individuals is probably 10 times more than that.

China has over 800,000 known immovable cultural relic sites above ground or underground. A total of 2,351 cultural sites are under national protection, 8,831 cultural sites under provincial-level protection and 58,371 under county-level protection. A national database on cultural relics will be completed and opened to the public by 2015.

Bronze Changxin Palace Lamp of the Han Dynasty

In the 1990s the Central Government earmarked some 700 million yuan for more than 1,000 cultural-relic preservation projects. As a result, large numbers of cultural relics were saved from destruction. Under a program launched in 2005, the state will provide 250 million yuan yearly for the protection of key relics nationwide.

Cultural relics have come under increasing legal protection too. China has signed four international treaties on relics preservation. The Law on the Protection of Cultural Relics, promulgated in 1982, institutes provisions on immovable cultural relics, archeological excavations, cultural relics preserved in

Censer of the Han Dynasty, plated with gold and silver

Ancient Hongcun Village, Anhui Province

museums, private collections, and the import and export of cultural relics. Implementation Regulations for the Law on the Protection of Cultural Relics and Provisional Regulations on the Administration of Relics Auction were issued in 2003. In 2006 the Measures of Beijing Municipality on the Protection of the Great Wall, the first special regulation, came into effect.

So far, the government has listed 110 famous historical and cultural cities under state protection, and over 80 under provincial-level protection. From 2001 an annual 15 million yuan has been allocated for their protection.

Traditionally an agricultural country, China has a large number of ancient villages. Their natural environment, as well as folk customs and handicrafts have been well preserved. A large-scale move to protect these ancient villages is being contemplated.

Intangible Cultural Heritage

China possesses a wealth of intangible cultural heritages. In June 2006 it released the first catalogue of 518 state-level intangible cultural heritage items in 10 categories of

Huishan clay figurines

folk literature, folk music, folk dance, traditional opera, *quyi*, acrobatics and competitive sports, folk art, traditional handicraft, traditional medicine and folk customs.

China's Kunqu Opera, art of playing the *guqin* (seven-stringed zither), Uyghur Muqam music and Mongolian pastoral songs have been included on the UNESCO list of Masterpieces of the Oral and Intangible Heritage of Humanity. In 2005, for the first time, China submitted a joint application with another country (Mongolia) for Mongolian pastoral songs to be entered on the list. The Chinese traditional music sound archives, records of the Qing Dynasty (1644-1911) Grand Secretariat, list of successful candidates in the Qing Dynasty imperial examinations, ancient records written in Naxi Dongba pictographs and Qing Dynasty architectural design archives of the Lei family have also been inscribed in the Memory of the World program. In 2001 the Tibetan epic *King Gesar*, the world's longest, was listed by the UNESCO in its world millennium memorials.

China has done a great deal of effective work on the protection of intangible cultural heritage items, including 10 Collections of China's Folk and Minority Cultures and Arts, a compilation of 300 volumes of nearly 500 million words, and saved and preserved numerous rare artistic and cultural resources. In February 2006 the State Council promulgated its Notice on Intensifying the Protection of

Intangible Cultural Heritage, giving detailed requirements regarding the survey, protection and rescue of intangible cultural heritage, the establishment of a regional listing at all levels and ultimately a national protection system.

Natural and Cultural Heritage

China joined the Convention for the Protection of the World Cultural and Natural Heritage in 1985, and began to submit applications in 1986. Now China has 41 cultural relics and natural spots included on the World Heritage List.

Since 2004 massive renovations have been made to Beijing's six cultural heritage sites – the Ming Tombs, the Great Wall, the Forbidden City, the Temple of Heaven, the Summer Palace and the Peking Man Site at Zhoukoudian. Beginning in 2006, China set the second Saturday of June as Cultural Heritage Day.

Yungang Grottoes, Shanxi Province

Peking Man site at Zhoukoudian

Mountain Resort and its outlying temples, Chengde

Ancient building complex in the Wudang Mountains

A classical garden of Suzhou

The Great Wall
Beijing, 1987, World Cultural Heritage

Imperial Palaces of the Ming and Qing Dynasties in Beijing and Shenyang
World Cultural Heritage: the Forbidden City, Beijing, 1987; Imperial Palace of the Qing Dynasty, Shenyang, Liaoning Province, 2004

Peking Man Site at Zhoukoudian
Beijing, 1987, World Cultural Heritage

Mogao Caves
Gansu Province, 1987, World Cultural Heritage

Mausoleum of the First Qin Emperor
Shaanxi Province, 1987, World Cultural Heritage

Mount Taishan
Shandong Province, 1987, World Cultural and Natural Heritage

Mount Huangshan
Anhui Province, 1990, World Cultural and Natural Heritage

Jiuzhaigou Valley Scenic and Historic Interest Area
Sichuan Province, 1992, World Natural Heritage

Huanglong Scenic and Historic Interest Area
Sichuan Province, 1992, World Natural Heritage

Wulingyuan Scenic and Historic Interest Area
Hunan Province, 1992, World Natural Heritage

Mountain Resort and Its Outlying Temples, Chengde
Hebei Province, 1994, World Cultural Heritage

Historic Ensemble of the Potala Palace, Lhasa
Tibet Autonomous Region, 1994, World Cultural Heritage

Temple and Cemetery of Confucius and the Kong Family Mansion in Qufu
Shandong Province, 1994, World Cultural Heritage

Ancient Building Complex in the Wudang Mountains
Hubei Province, 1994, World Cultural Heritage

Lushan National Park
Jiangxi Province, 1996, World Cultural Heritage

Mount Emei Scenic Area, Including Leshan Giant Buddha Scenic Area
Sichuan Province, 1996, World Cultural and Natural Heritage

Ancient City of Pingyao
Shanxi Province, 1997, World Cultural Heritage

Classical Gardens of Suzhou
Jiangsu Province, 1997, World Cultural Heritage

Old Town of Lijiang
Yunnan Province, 1997, World Cultural Heritage

Summer Palace, an Imperial Garden in Beijing
Beijing, 1998, World Cultural Heritage

Temple of Heaven, an Imperial Sacrificial Altar in Beijing
Beijing, 1998, World Cultural Heritage

Mount Wuyi
Fujian Province, 1999, World Cultural and Natural Heritage

Dazu Rock Carvings
Chongqing, 1999, World Cultural Heritage

Imperial Tombs of the Ming and Qing Dynasties
World Cultural Heritage: Ming Xianling Mausoleum, Hubei Province, 2000; Qing Dongling Mausoleum and Qing Xiling Mausoleum, Hebei Province, 2000; Ming Tombs, Beijing, 2003; Ming Xiaoling Mausoleum, Jiangsu Province, 2003; three imperial mausoleums of Shengjing, Liaoning Province, 2004

Longmen Grottoes
Henan Province, 2000, World Cultural Heritage

Mount Qingcheng and the Dujiangyan Irrigation System
Sichuan Province, 2000, World Cultural Heritage

Ancient Villages in Southern Anhui — Xidi and Hongcun
Anhui Province, 2000, World Cultural Heritage

Summer Palace, an imperial garden in Beijing

An imperial tomb of the Qing Dynasty

Mount Qingcheng

Fujian Tulou

Danxia landscape on the border between Hunan Province and Guangxi Zhuang Autonomous Region

Yungang Grottoes
Shanxi Province, 2001, World Cultural Heritage

Three Parallel Rivers of Yunnan Protected Areas
Yunnan Province, 2003, World Natural Heritage

Capital Cities and Tombs of the Ancient Koguryo Kingdom
Liaoning and Jilin Provinces, 2004, World Cultural Heritage

Historic Center of Macao
Macao Special Administrative Region, 2005, World Cultural Heritage

Yin Xu
Henan Province, 2006, World Cultural Heritage

Sichuan Giant Panda Sanctuaries
Sichuan Province, 2006, World Natural Heritage

Kaiping Diaolou and Villages
Guangdong Province, 2007, World Cultural Heritage

South China Karst
Yunnan Province, Guizhou Province and Chongqing Municipality, 2007, World Natural Heritage

Fujian Tulou
Fujian Province, 2008, World Cultural Heritage

Mount Sanqingshan National Park
Jiangxi Province, 2008, World Natural Heritage

Mount Wutai
Shanxi Province, 2009, World Cultural Heritage

Historic Monuments of Dengfeng in "The Center of Heaven and Earth"
Henan Province, 2010, World Cultural Heritage

China Danxia
Chishui, Guizhou Province; Taining, Fujian Province; Langshan, Hunan Province; Mount Danxia, Guangdong Province; Mount Longhu, Jiangxi Province; Mount Jianglang, Zhejiang Province, 2010, World Natural Heritage

West Lake Cultural Landscape of Hangzhou
Zhejiang Province, 2011, World Cultural Heritage

Literature

The Book of Songs, China's first anthology of poems and earliest literary achievement, was compiled in the 6th century BC. The literature composed in the long succession of dynasties that followed includes pre-Qin prose in a simple style, magnificent Han-dynasty *fu* (rhymed prose) and *yuefu* (folk songs) of the late Han. The Tang Dynasty alone is credited with thousands of poets, including Li Bai and Du Fu, who together left more than 50,000 poems. The Song Dynasty was known for its *ci* (lyrics), and the Yuan Dynasty for *zaju* (poetic drama set to music). The Ming and Qing dynasties saw the production of four masterpiece novels: *Three Kingdoms*, *Outlaws of the Marsh*, *Journey to the West* and *A Dream of Red Mansions*.

The development of modern Chinese literature has seen two golden ages: the 1920s and 1930s, and the 1980s and 1990s. The first heyday, starting with the New Culture Movement, demonstrated strong opposition to imperialism and feudalism. Progressive writers, exemplified by Lu Xun, pioneered China's modern literature. Lu Xun, Shen Congwen, Ba Jin, Mao Dun, Lao She, Ding Ling and (Eileen) Zhang Ailing have since come to be regarded as modern masters of Chinese literature.

The emergence in the 1980s and 1990s of a number of more internationally influential writers and works reflects the achievements and richness of China's late-20th century literature.

A Dream of Red Mansions, Three Kingdoms, Outlaws of the Marsh and *Journey to the West* are the four most famous classical novels in China.

Writers showed greater maturity in the use of contemporary language to express the lives and aesthetic experiences of modern Chinese people. Generally speaking, the artistry of thought and literary expression achieved by contemporary novelists surpassed that of the previous generation.

China has dozens of literary awards, the most prestigious of which are the Mao Dun Literary Award, the Lu Xun Literary Award, and the annual Zhonghua Literary Figure of the Year. The Chinese Women's Literary Awards, the presentation of which is held every five years, is a major national award scheme covering works

Online Literature Clubs

Online literature clubs provide literature fans with more works to enjoy and space to show their literary talents than traditional literature agencies. Well-known online literature clubs in China include China Internet Literature Federation, www.baifan.net, www.qidian.com, www.ssyz.net, Yamo Literature Society and www.diliubi.com.

by women in the fields of novels, prose, poetry, documentary writing, women's literary theory and translation.

In 1995 China's first literature website "The Olive Tree" was established. The explosion of Internet literature has become the latest eye-catching phenomenon for China's literature. As a new medium for literature, Internet literature is growing rapidly and greatly influencing the general pattern of Chinese literature as a whole. In 2002 the emergence of www.qidian.com, affiliated to Shanda Interactive Entertainment Ltd, signaled that access to Internet literature was not free any more. In 2006 the popularization of the blogosphere stirred up another wave of publication of Internet literature. Internet literature, due to its huge commercial value, has become the industry with the most potential among China's cultural and creative endeavors.

Opera

Chinese traditional opera, Greek drama and Indian Sanskrit opera are considered to be the world's three most ancient opera forms. China boasts more than 300 types of local operas, including Peking Opera, Kunqu Opera, Shaoxing Opera, Henan Opera, Guangdong Opera, Sichuan Opera and Shaanxi Opera. Among them, Peking Opera is the most popular and influential. Chinese traditional opera mainly expresses stories through song and dance forms. The Plum Blossom Award is the highest prize for young and middle-aged opera performers.

Modern drama was introduced to China in the early 20th century, and came of age in the 1930s. The Beijing People's Art Theater, founded

Peking Opera

Peking Opera is China's representative opera. Over the last 200 years it has developed a repertoire of more than 1,000 works, as well as special sets of musical genres and stylized performance movements. Famous Peking Opera artists, including Mei Lanfang, Cheng Yanqiu, Ma Lianliang and Zhou Xinfang, emerged in the last century, and new artists continue to emerge in the 21st century.

Kunqu

Kunqu Opera has a history of more than 500 years. It is a representative opera of the Ming and Qing dynasties. Listed as one of the Masterpieces of the Oral and Intangible Heritage of Humanity, Kunqu epitomizes the aesthetic beauty of Chinese opera. Kunqu performances feature powerful lyricism, exquisite acting and elegant tunes. The classic repertoire includes *The Peony Pavilion* and *Palace of Eternal Youth*.

Making up for a traditional Chinese opera

in 1952, represents the apex of Chinese theater. The Theater has staged nearly 100 dramas, among which *Teahouse* enjoys international prestige as a classical drama. The late Cao Yu is considered China's best modern dramatist.

Quyi

Quyi is the name for traditional Chinese spoken and singing arts. It is a unique form of art developed over a long history from folk oral literature and song. There are about 400 *quyi* genres, including comic dialogues, Beijing musical storytelling with drum accompaniment, Yangzhou ditties, Shandong musical storytelling with clappers, Anhui musical storytelling, song-and-dance duets popular in northeast China and Fengyang flower-drum performance. Comic dialogues and storytelling are the most widespread genres, commonly performed on radio, TV and the stage.

Music

As far back as the first century BC there were over 80 Chinese musical instruments. Ancient musical works still extant include *Guangling Melody* and *Eighteen*

Scene from a traditional Chinese opera

Pipa, Chinese lute

Erhu, a two-stringed Chinese fiddle

Bamboo flute

Guqin, a traditional Chinese zither

Stanzas for the Barbarian Reed Pipe played on the *guqin* (zither), *Ambush from All Sides* played on the *pipa* (lute) and *Spring Flowers on a Moonlit Night on the River* played by a traditional wind and stringed instrument orchestra.

Since the middle of the 20th century, along with the introduction of Western music and musical instruments, Chinese music has made great progress. Chinese musicians have created a number of outstanding works with national characteristics, including *The East Is Red*, a large-scale music and dance epic; *The Red Guards on Honghu Lake*, an opera; and *The Yellow River Concerto*, for piano. Chinese musicians and art performance troupes have participated in a variety of international exchanges and competitions, and won many prizes.

Large-scale music festivals are held regularly – for example, the annual Shanghai International Art Festival, Beijing International Music Festival and Beijing International Opera Season. They attract a large number of world-famous musicians and top-level music and art troupes.

Dance

Chinese folk dancing has a long history, with the country's 56 ethnic groups creating many dances with unique characteristics, such as the northern Han people's *yangge* dance, south China's tea-picking lantern dance, the Mongolian *andai* dance and the Tibetan *xuanzi* dance.

In 1959 the National Ballet of China was founded, introducing Western ballet to China. Ballets with Chinese characteristics, such as *The Red Detachment of Women*, *The White-haired Girl* and *Raise the Red Lantern*, enjoy wide popularity. During festivals, folk dancing is a popular form of entertainment; while national song and dance troupes, such as China Opera and Ballet Theater, China Oriental Song and Dance Troupe, China National Ethnic Song and Dance Ensemble and National Ballet of China provide professional, high-standard performances. The dance drama *The Peony Pavilion* combines classic essence and modern elements.

A festival dance show

吟徵調高篇下桐
松間疑有入松風
仰窺低審含情客
以聽無紘一再中
臣京謹題

Calligraphy and Painting

Chinese written characters are square-shaped, with an emphasis on vigor of style and structure. The art of calligraphy developed naturally from China's unique writing system. Every dynasty had its great calligraphers whose styles came to represent their times, and the Chinese people's love of calligraphy is still fresh today.

Different from Western oil painting, traditional Chinese painting is characterized by unique forms of expression. Its roots can be traced back to paintings on Neolithic pottery 6,000 to 7,000 years ago. Since similar tools were used to draw lines for the earliest painting and writing, painting and calligraphy are said to share the same origin. Chinese paintings often include poems and/or calligraphy. They also often bear the seals of their various owners. Thus the four art forms are integrated, providing a richer aesthetic experience. Figure, landscape, and flower-and-bird paintings are the

Listening to the Zither, said to have been painted by Emperor Huizong of the Song Dynasty (960-1279)

major traditional painting genres, with masterpieces of different genres emerging in different dynasties.

Contemporary painting and calligraphy are still flourishing. The National Art Museum of China and similar bodies hold individual or joint exhibitions every year, and many exhibitions of traditional Chinese painting have been held overseas. Chinese artists have also made remarkable

798 Art Zone

Situated in the northeast suburbs of Beijing, the 798 Art Zone was previously the site of state-owned electronics factories, including the biggest factory numbered "798." In 2002 groups of artists and cultural organizations began to move in, turning the area into a complex for galleries, art centers, artists' studios, design companies, cafes and restaurants. Similar to New York's Soho district, with artists living in lofts, the 798 Art Zone has become an exhibition center for Chinese art and culture, especially avant-garde art.

Folk Arts and Crafts

China boasts a wide variety of arts and crafts renowned for excellent workmanship. In terms of technique, Chinese folk arts are categorized into cutting, bundling, plaiting, knitting, embroidering, carving, molding, and painting. They have strong local flavor and diverse folk styles. Special arts and crafts involve the use of precious or special materials, combined with elaborate designs and processes to produce works of great elegance. For example, jade carving uses jadestone raw material; Jingtai cloisonné enamel gets its name from the Jingtai reign (1450-1457) of the Ming Dynasty, from blue glaze on copper filament, which after polishing reveals magnificence in design and color.

Cloisonné enamel work

Jackie Chan and Zhang Ziyi at the First Beijing International Film Festival, April 2011

progress in Western-style oil painting, woodcuts and watercolors; and many have created works that combine traditional Chinese and Western techniques, adding brilliance to both forms. With various kinds of modern materials, forms, frameworks and genres, excellent modern artworks continue to emerge. New media artworks, including video, digital, animated and audio art, are now commonly seen at domestic and overseas exhibitions.

Cinema

China has become the world' third largest movie producer and No.1 TV drama producer, with movie box-office sales increasing by over 30% for the past six consecutive years.

Realism has remained the mainstream of Chinese cinema. In the wave of film-making that rose in the mid-1980s realistic works reached high levels of creativity in varied subject matters, styles and forms, and in the exploration and innovation

Cartoon poster

Animations and Cartoons

China's 367 million minors are the consumer group with the most potential for the animation and cartoon industry, the market which is worth over 100 billion yuan every year. In July 2004 China National Center for Developing the Animation, Cartoon & Video Game Industry was established in Shanghai. By the end of the same year, three satellite channels specializing in animation and cartoon works were given approval, including Beijing KAKU Cartoon Channel, Shanghai Toonmax Cartoon Satellite TV, and Hunan Golden Eagle Cartoon Satellite TV. Nine national centers for animation and cartoon works and four teaching and research centers for animation training were established. China International Cartoon and Animation Festival has been held annually since 2005.

of cinematic language. Chinese directors, including Zhang Yimou, Chen Kaige and Huang Jianxin, rose to fame during this period, becoming international cinema celebrities. The late 1990s saw the emergence of directors like Jia Zhangke, Wang Xiaoshuai, Zhang Yuan and Lou Ye, who were mostly born in the 1960s and 1970s. Their movies portray ordinary people's lives in a realistic fashion.

The Changchun and Shanghai international film festivals are annual events. The "Golden Rooster" is the top prize for Chinese movies. The government has established the "Huabiao Awards" especially to encourage the mainstream movies. The "Hundred Flowers Awards" are presented on the basis of audience votes. Many other awards also contribute to the development of China's movies, including the Golden Calf Awards for Children's Movies, Hong Kong Film Awards, Golden Bauhinia Awards, Taiwan Golden Horse Awards and Chinese Movie Media Awards.

Mass Media

Online Media

The population of netizens in China has reached 420 million, as Internet service now covers 99.3% of towns and 91.5% of administrative villages. Some 96.3% of the towns now have broadband access, and the 3G network basically covers the whole country. The online media provides the most convenient platform for enlarging information sources and increasing transparency in society.

Online Governance Consultation

With its increasing popularization, the Internet is becoming a major channel for Chinese citizens to implement their right to know, right to participate, right to express opinions and right to supervise. On June 20, 2008 President Hu Jintao held an online conversation with netizens through www.people.com. cn. Civil servants communicate with the people via the Internet on government policies, making government information more transparent and accessible. Since the micro blog came into being in 2009, it has become the third information source on the Internet following the news and forums.

Since the mid-1990s China's traditional media has joined hands with online media and developed their businesses online. Popular news websites are playing a unique role in news dissemination.

After China Mobile launched its cell-phone TV service in 2005, news images and text became available on mobile phones, prompting a spate of news websites to also provide cell-phone reports. In August 2006 the General Administration of Press and Publications launched a project to explore forms of digital publication and the operating modes of online, cell-phone and electronic newspapers.

The latest trend in China's media industry is to form intermedia and transregional media operating on multiple patterns. In 2001 the government set a goal of establishing transregional multimedia news groups, and instituted detailed regulations on fund-raising, foreign cooperation and trans-media expansion to this end. The China Radio, Film and TV Group, founded in late 2001, is now China's largest and most powerful multimedia group, covering television, the Internet, publishing and advertising, through integrating the resources of national radio, TV and film organizations, along with those of Internet firms. CCTV's English channel reaches US audiences via News Group's Fox News network.

The billboard of the group-purchase website lashou.com

Public telephone booth with WIFI access

The microblog booth at the 3rd Global Mobile Internet Conference

Newspapers

The total and daily circulation of China's daily newspapers have taken the leading position in the world, with a total circulation of nearly 50 billion copies and average circulation per day over 100 million copies. Newspapers feature diversified forms to cater to different reader groups.

Recent years have seen a trend of reorganization of newspapers. To date, nearly 50 newspaper groups have been established, including Beijing Daily Group, Wenhui-Xinmin United Press Group and Guangzhou Daily Press Group. In 2006 Tianjin Daily News Group adopted digital technology in its distribution and, via satellite transmission, began serving immediate-printing and real-time reading of its *Tianjin Daily* in 39 countries.

The influence and competitiveness of newspapers are weakening in the face of the growing popularity of radio, television and the Internet. To compete with the electronic media, the newspaper world is shifting from sole news function to opinion and service functions, providing online and mobile phone newspapers while remaining the traditional form. With an electric layout via mobile reading terminals like iPad, the newspapers could continue their traditional procedures of interviewing and editing, layout and business mode.

Radio

China National Radio, China's official radio station, has 13 channels broadcasting 260 hours of programs per day via satellite. Every province, autonomous region and municipality also has its own radio station.

China Radio International (CRI) is the only state radio station targeting overseas audiences. It has 2,471 hours of programs beamed daily across the globe in 51 foreign languages, in addition to standard Chinese (*putonghua*), four Chinese dialects and 5 Chinese ethnic-minority languages.

Television

China's television industry has a complete system with program production, transmission and coverage. China Central Television (CCTV), the state station, has 21 open-circuit channels, one high-definition channel, over 20 digital payment channels and 28 online channels that broadcast over 630 hours of programs each day. In addition, every province, autonomous region and municipality has its own TV station.

China Network Television (CNTV) started broadcasting on December 28, 2009. CNTV has 450,000 hours of videos and assembles TV programs totaling over 1,000 hours from TV stations nationwide. It has done pioneering work in the field of digital preservation of historical and cultural items.

China Xinhua News Network Corporation (CNC) is a television station sponsored by Xinhua News Agency. Its Chinese- and English-language channels broadcast news programs 24 hours a day, covering world news ranging from emergencies to important political, economic and cultural events. As an international new TV agency,

the CNC broadcasts programs to the Asia-Pacific area, North America, Europe, the Middle East and Africa through satellite, cable, cell phone and online TV.

Large international expositions, including the Shanghai TV Festival, Beijing International TV Week, China Radio and TV Expo and Sichuan TV Festival, are held on a regular basis. Besides judging entries and conferring awards, these festivals conduct academic exchanges and import and export of TV programs.

Publishing

Since the introduction of the reform and opening-up policy 30 years ago, China has witnessed a transformation from a "book desert" to a "book ocean," and the mushrooming of millions of publications, and the mode of communication has changed from paper media alone to multimedia.

The number of books and magazines published in China leads the world, with a total of 7.037 billion copies of 310,000 titles of books – up from 12,900 titles in 1977 – and 3.153 billion copies of 9,851 magazines.

More than 100 press and publishing groups have been established across the country, with 45 listed on the stock market. It is estimated that the sales amount of China's digital publications will account for 50% of the total of the whole publishing industry by 2020, and 90% of books will have online counterparts by 2030.

In line with China's WTO commitments, the General Administration of Press and Publications in May 2003 promulgated its Administrative Measures for Foreign-invested Book, Newspaper and Periodical Distribution Enterprises, allowing foreign investors to engage in publication retailing as of May 1, 2003, and wholesaling from December 1, 2004. But the Administration's approval is required for any such retail or wholesale organization to be opened.

> **"China Book International"**
>
> In 2006 the Information Office of the State Council, together with the General Administration of Press and Publications, commenced "China Book International." In 2009 the Information Office announced more financial support to publishers around the world for translating and publishing books on China in the international market in order to present a complete and real China to readers worldwide.

Digital publishing is booming in China.

Appendix I

Completion of the 11th Five-year Plan

2006-2010

Some 86.4% of the targets set in the 11th Five-year Plan (2006-2010) were fulfilled, remarkably higher than the 64.3% in the 10th Five-year Plan (2001-2005) and the 75% in the Ninth Five-year Plan (1996-2000). However, the problem of unbalanced, inconsistent and unsustainable development remains unsolved. To achieve comprehensive, balanced and sustainable economic and social development, China will continue to shoulder heavy responsibilities for a long time to come.

The 11th Five-year Plan

One of the best accomplished five-year plans in history

Targets accomplishment rate

The 11th Five-year Plan	86.4%
The 10th Five-year Plan	64.3%
The Ninth Five-year Plan	75%

Eight targets concerning the people's well-being all achieved

By the end of the 11th Five-year Plan period, the per-capita income	Urban 19,109 yuan
	Rural 5,919 yuan

Economic growth steadily improved

During the 11th Five-year Plan period, China's average annual economic growth rate was over 11%

Over-fulfilling the target of 7.5% set in the Plan

Targets of energy saving and emissions reduction basically realized

Eight targets concerning population, resources and the environment were basically achieved.

Persistent structural adjustment

China's current urbanization rate: 47.5%

By the end of the 10th Five-year Plan period (2001-2005): 43%

Source: Xinhua News Agency

People's well-being targets fulfilled, but new problems remain

Improving the people's well-being was the focus of the 11th Five-year Plan: Eight of the total 22 targets were about public services and the people's life, of which two obligatory ones were included in a Five-year Plan for the first time. During the transformation of a growth-oriented government into a public-service-oriented (people's well-being-oriented) one, the Chinese government has applied more manpower, material and financial resources to improve the people's well-being.

By the end of 2010 eight targets concerning the people's well-being had been achieved: Urban and rural residents' income had increased by a large margin; free nine-year compulsory education had been comprehensively realized; the coverage rates of urban basic pension insurance and new rural cooperative medical care had reached their goals ahead of schedule; and the urban employed population had increased by 55 million....

Nevertheless, as a developing country, China's social programs still lag behind its economic growth, with newly emerging problems to be solved urgently.

Economic growth improved dramatically, characterized by continuously enhanced sustainability

During the 11th Five-year Plan period, China maintained an average annual economic growth rate of over 11%, compared to the target of 7.5%.

The 11th Five-year Plan had a smooth start, with the first two years' economic growth rates over 10%. In spite of the sharp economic decline during the global financial crisis, the Chinese government adopted economic stimulus package plans and made guiding adjustments to macro-control policies in a timely fashion to promote economic recovery.

To China as a large developing country, development is imperative. Especially while addressing the global financial crisis, China has to maintain sound economic growth so as to increase enterprise profits and the employment rate. Currently, its economy is still restricted by problems with resources and the environment, and faces other newly emerging problems.

Energy saving and emission reductions basically achieved, despite continuously growing difficulties

Five years ago, energy saving and emissions reduction, as an obligatory target, was included for the first time in the 11th Five-year Plan: per-unit GDP energy consumption to be reduced by 20%, and gross emissions of major pollutants to be reduced by 10%. By the end of 2010, the total eight targets concerning population, resources and environment including the two items mentioned above, had been basically achieved.

It was not easy to achieve these results, especially those regarding energy conservation, previously set according to a predicted annual GDP growth rate of 7.5% (which actually exceeded 11%). During the 11th Five-year Plan period, China's gross energy conservation reached 600 million tons of standard coal equivalent, which is equal to a CO_2 emissions reduction of over 1.5 billion tons. This has not only relieved the pressure of resource shortage and environmental damage on China, but also proved to be a significant contribution to addressing global climate change.

Structural adjustments proceeding comparatively slowly with scrupulous planning

By weeding out overcapacity and backward productivity, developing strategic emerging industries, expanding domestic demand, and instituting regional economic development plans over the past five years, in spite of the impact of the global financial crisis and natural disasters, China had been persistent in adjusting and optimizing its economic structure.

China's urbanization rate has increased to 47.5% – from 43% in the 10th Five-year Plan period. In the 11th Plan years China invested hugely in R&D, and tertiary industry developed rapidly, but "service industry growth proportion and employment proportion" and "research and experiment expenditure proportion of the GDP" lagged behind.

In the 12th Five-year Plan, strategic economic restructuring will be the direction for accelerating the transformation of the economic development mode, and detailed plans have been made accordingly.

Appendix II
Some Commonly Used Websites

Chinese Government
http://english.gov.cn

Ministry of Foreign Affairs
http://www.fmprc.gov.cn/eng

Information Office of State Council
http://www.scio.gov.cn

News Agencies
Xinhua News Agency
http://www.chinaview.cn

China News Agency
http://www.chinanews.com

TV
CCTV
http://english.cctv.com

Broadcast
China Radio International
http://english.cri.cn

External Publicity
China International Publishing Group
http://www.cipg.org.cn

China International
Communication Center
http://www.cicc.org.cn

China Internet Information Center
http://www.china.org.cn

China Development Gateway
http://en.chinagate.com.cn

Newspapers
People's Daily
http://english.peopledaily.com.cn

China Daily
http://chinadaily.com.cn

Magazines
Beijing Review
http://www.bjreview.com.cn

China Today
http://www.chinatoday.com.cn

China Pictorial
http://www.rmhb.com.cn/chpic/
htdocs/english/

Women of China
http://www.womenofchina.com.cn

Books

Foreign Languages Press
http://www.flp.com.cn

New World Press
http://www.nwp.com.cn

Sinolingua
http://www.sinolingua.com.cn

Morning Glory Press
http://210.72.20.211:3042/main/

Dolphin Books
http://www.dolphin-books.com.cn

China Pictorial Publishing House
http://www.zghbcbs.com

New Star Press
http://www.newstarpress.com

China Intercontinental Press
http://www.cicc.org.cn

International Publication Distribution

China International Book
Trading Corporation
http://www.cibtc.com.cn/gtweb/
new_enhome.do

Travel Agencies

China International Travel
Service Head Office
http://www.cits.cn

China Travel Service Head Office
http://www.ctsho.com

China Youth Travel Service Tours
Holding Co., Ltd
http://www.cytsonline.com

China Comfort Travel Co., Ltd
http://www.cct.cn

CITIC Travel Co., Ltd
http://www.travel.citic.com

China Women Travel Service
http://www.cwts.com.cn

China Peace International Tourism
Co., Ltd
http://www.hply.com

图书在版编目（CIP）数据

中国. 2011：英文 / 钟欣 编；外文出版社英文编译部译.
—北京：外文出版社，2011
ISBN 978-7-119-07180-0

Ⅰ.①中… Ⅱ.①钟… ②外… Ⅲ.①社会主义建设成就
–中国–2011–英文 Ⅳ.①D619

中国版本图书馆CIP数据核字（2011）第140502号

撰　　稿：崔黎丽　潘　灯　王传民　王奎庭　王振红　熊冰颐 等
图　　片：新华社图片社　CFP　人民画报社　CNS　CTPS
　　　　　Bernardo De Niz　Bobby Brill　陈林峰　陈顺国　陈卫东　邓　佳
　　　　　杜泽泉　方东风　高　勇　胡卫国　黄君毅　金建潮　兰佩瑾　李　丹
　　　　　李　林　李　涓　李茂达　李显波　刘春根　楼庆西　Lowell Bennett
　　　　　陆　敏　罗文发　马井生　茹遂初　孙剑江　孙树明　孙永学
　　　　　徐子翘　杨逸畴　伊　海　银道禄　游云谷　俞　亮　虞向军
　　　　　郁向阳　王　磊　王　涛　吴卫东　张　锷　张书奇　张顺春　曾向强
中文审定：萧师铃
文图审定：徐明强
英文翻译：王　琴　姜晓宁　王　玮　刘奎娟　严　晶　曲　磊　冯　鑫
英文审定：Paul White　韩清月
责任编辑：蔡莉莉　文　芳
地图制作：北京好山河文化发展有限公司
审 图 号：GS（2011）763号
装帧设计：北京凤焉图文设计工作室
印刷监制：冯　浩

中　国

钟　欣 编

出版发行：外文出版社有限责任公司
地　　址：中国北京西城区百万庄大街24号　　　邮政编码：100037
网　　址：http:// www.flp.com.cn　　　　　　　电子邮箱：flp@cipg.org.cn
电　　话：008610-68320579（总编室）　　008610-68327750（版权部）
　　　　　008610-68995852（发行部）　　008610-68996158（编辑部）
印　　制：外文印刷厂
开　　本：889mm×1194mm　1/32
印　　张：7.25
版　　次：2011年9月第1版第1次印刷
书　　号：ISBN 978-7-119-07180-0
09900（英）（平装）